How to l  as a **Bodyguard**

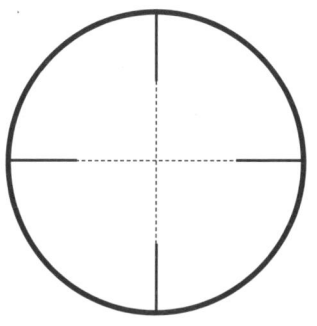

How to Find Work as a Bodyguard

A Guide to Personal Protection

Robin Barratt

Introduction by
Stuart Bridges
Member of the Association of British Investigators

Robin Barratt

How to Find Work as a Bodyguard

This edition published by Varsity Publications
PO Box 222, Chipping Norton, Oxford OX7 5WY, UK

Telephone + 44 (0)870 350 1231 Fax: + 44 (0)870 1241
E-mail: varsityox@aol.com   Website: www.varsitypublications.com

© Copyright Varsity Publications 2004
ISBN: 0 946981 32 9

No part of this publication may be reproduced, stored in a retrieval system or transmitted in any form or by any means electronic, electrostatic, magnetic tape, mechanical, photocopying, or otherwise without the express permission in writing from the copyright holder.

Typesetting & Page Layout by: Laserset, Abingdon, Oxon, UK. Tel: (01235) 529423
Printed by: Athenaeum Press Ltd, Gateshead, Tyne & Wear, UK. Tel: (0191) 491 0770

The Publishers regret that while every effort has been made during the compilation of this publication to ensure the accuracy of information obtained and published, they cannot be held responsible in any way for inaccuracies in the information supplied to them for publication, or obtained from other sources, nor for accidental errors or omissions.

The information contained in this publication has been compiled through research and personal experience and no charge has been levied from any individual, company or organization mentioned. Inclusion of a company or individual should not be interpreted as a recommendation of that company or individual, and the publishers offer no comment on the ability of any company or individual listed to undertake particular assignments. Similarly, no criticism is implied of any company or individual who may for any reason have been omitted from this Publication.

The views contained herein are solely the views and opinions of the author.

CONTENTS

Introduction 7

Foreword 9

A Little Bit of History 11

Chapter One "Are you really up to it?" 13

Chapter Two "Training" 23

Chapter Three "New UK Laws" .29

Chapter Four "Your CV" 37

Chapter Five "Starting your own company" 51

Chapter Six "How to get work" .55

Chapter Seven "Starting up overseas" 63

Chapter Eight "Diversifying" 69

Chapter Nine "The Contract of Employment" 73

Chapter Ten - "Frequently Asked Questions" 77

Contacts List 83

INTRODUCTION

Welcome to this new Edition of Robin Barratt's *"How to Find Work as a Bodyguard"*. His manual on close protection was originally published in 2003 by Diverse Publications Ltd but we are now delighted to add it to the range of Varsity books specifically aimed at the security and related industries.

Robin has written a truthful and totally unbiased aid for the prospective bodyguard, telling it exactly as it is. His book is an invaluable guide for anyone looking to work in the tough, hard world of personal protection – whether as an individual or as a company, whether they are just starting out or fairly experienced, it will prove invaluable.

The book covers all aspects of the industry, detailing how to effectively present your CV or company profile, what training and experiences prospective employers are looking for, who are the main employers, whom to approach and how to approach them, advice and information on forming your own bodyguard company and how to market and establish yourself overseas. An extra chapter has been added to cover the new UK laws affecting the private security industry, and throughout the narrative Robin has included a series of case histories as well as a comprehensive question and answer forum. The manual finishes with a list of useful international contacts.

Robin Barratt, who is currently based in Moscow, has spent over 15 years in the industry, and the wide knowledge he has acquired during that time has been distilled into this highly effective but entertaining book. He was a founder member of the Worldwide Federation of Bodyguards and has worked extensively as a bodyguard in high risk environments, including Russia, Bosnia, Israel and Africa. Robin has also provided training for bodyguards around the world and has written books and numerous articles on this subject.

I hope you will enjoy reading this new edition of Robin Barratt's Bodyguard Manual and that you will be helped and encouraged by the sound, sensible and easy-to-follow advice it contains.

Stuart C. Bridges, BA, Editor
Member of the Assoc of British Investigators
Varsity Publications, Oxford, May 2004

The author – Robin Barratt

FOREWORD

I started my first bodyguard assignment back in 1988 and have been working in the industry almost continually ever since. I have worked around the world and on contracts lasting from one day to over six months. I have experienced both the horror of war and assassination and the luxury of the executive lifestyle of the rich. Over the past 15 years I have had hundreds, if not thousands of CVs sent to me and have spoken to a huge amount of protection officers worldwide, from the fresh faced newly trained novice to the veteran. Each and every one full of enthusiasm, drive and all of them determined to succeed. Sadly almost everyone starting out in this industry eventually gives up. But those who don't - those who persevere, are dedicated and willing to work extremely hard can ultimately travel the world protecting the rich and the famous. It really is possible for those with fortitude and the willpower to succeed to have a wonderful career.

There is work out there, a lot of work. Western Europeans and Americans have never felt more vulnerable and have never been more concerned about their personal security and safety than they do in this present climate of extremism and terror. Since the 11th September the world has changed, and will continue to change. Life will never be the same and security is now a prime factor in almost everyone's daily life.

When putting this publication together I thought carefully about many things specifically relating to this industry. The first thing I decided, above everything is, is to tell it how it is. I am not going to bullsh*t or bluff; I will tell you why most people are unsuccessful at finding work and I will tell you what those who have been successful have done to achieve their success. I hope to give you ideas and tips, suggestions and information, which will arm you for that long road ahead. And for most of you it will be a long road.

I certainly do not profess to know it all. There are many out there with a great deal more experience than myself, but I feel have had more experience than most and have 15 years in the industry as proof of some sort of ability to stay working and earning a living from this business. Admittedly there have been a few extremely difficult times, but generally things have not been too bad and I am still here, living and working in one of the most violent cities in the world - Moscow.

Throughout this publication I will give examples of real life situations of what and what not to do. They are examples only; it doesn't mean that if you practise and follow everything I suggest you will find work. Everyone is different, but hopefully this publication will help a little.

Over the years I have come to the conclusion there really is only one main and very straightforward reason why most people are not successful and eventually give up. It is because, quite simply, they are not willing to do what is necessary to become successful. "Rubbish", I hear you cry. "I am willing to do anything to get work", but if you were, you would be out working and not reading this. In the forthcoming chapters I will explain exactly what you need to do, and I can almost guarantee that 99.9% of those reading this will not even attempt to do what I suggest. It takes dedication and commitment, and some form of financial investment, which most of you are not willing to take. Most of you, sadly, think that by attending a brief CP training course you are qualified to protect. Most of you are sadly wrong.

Being responsible for protecting someone against terror and assassination requires infinitely more than a ten-day training course. This publication isn't aimed at those wishing to work as an occasional minder to a rock star at a pop concert, or looking after a boxer at a boxing match, it is aimed at the international executive protection officer - where you really are employed as a bodyguard - in literally every single sense of the word.

Good luck and keep safe

Semper Vigians !!

Robin Barratt
May 2004 - Moscow

A LITTLE BIT OF HISTORY

Along with actors, prostitutes, soldiers and politicians, bodyguarding is said to be one of the oldest professions in the world. Bodyguards as such were not actually mentioned in the Bible but it is widely believed that there were protection specialists well before the birth of Christ. The first time professional bodyguards were mentioned in history was in 400 AD when the Anglo-Saxons invaded Great Britain. The Anglo-Saxons brought fear to the people and rulers of the country, and to protect local chieftains against the invaders teams of "bodyguards" were employed. These personal guards, known as comitati were honour-bound to defend the chieftain, even unto death. One recorded episode chronicling the bravery of the comitatus occurred in 991AD when the Vikings were camped off the coast of Britain, waiting for the tide to drop thus revealing a sand causeway to the shore. The local chieftain led his personal army along with his comitati to the causeway and defied the Vikings to cross. The chieftain, his soldiers and his comitati were heavily outnumbered. During the bloody battle the chieftain was killed yet his comitati continued fighting until they too were slain.

During the Middle Ages, very few church dignitaries travelled without their personal protection. Church dignitaries were probably the first to seek protection; they had their own cadre of guards and the Catholic Church had its own protection facilities and its own armies. Politicians were probably the first to utilize private bodyguards and, as more and more people developed wealth, the need for protection grew.

In Japan during 1100 AD, a feudal culture evolved where Lords built private castles and kingdoms and recruited their own armies, with the most trusted of their military personnel becoming their personal guards. It was the time of the Shogun, where the Japanese Samurai were honour-bound to protect their daimyo's life and territory. The Samurai culture lasted for hundreds of years and honour was a deeply held conviction for members of this society. It was the time of the Bushido Code, the time of giri. The Samurai held a rigid and tight code of honour, a code of obligation. For a Samurai to betray his sense of honour meant complete loss of face which could only be atoned for by seppuku - the honourable and ritualistic method of suicide. Here the do-shai - the shorter of the two swords carried by a warrior - would be plunged into the left side of the stomach, drawn through the body from left to right, and then a harsh final thrust upward. The Samurai's most trusted lieutenant, or closest friend, would act as his second. He would stand ready with his katana (the long sword) drawn and it was his duty to decapitate the Samurai before he could show pain and disgrace himself.

During the end of the fifteenth century the ronin, a group of forty seven Samurai pretended to live without giri, that is without honour, without obligation after their master was forced to commit seppuku. They pretended to live in disgrace until the time came when they sought revenge for the injustice that had taken their Master's life. After purposely losing their giri, they maintained their oath to their Lord and eventually avenged his death, regaining their honour. Eventually the term ronin became synonymous with outlaw. Some historians believe the ronin became the very first ninjas. The forty-seven ronin are honoured even to this day in Japan.

Personal bodyguards have been recruited and chosen throughout history for their skills, knowledge, power, and of course their honour. Any person interested in becoming a personal bodyguard should consider the questions of "honour."

CHAPTER ONE

ARE YOU REALLY UP TO IT?

This is certainly going to be the hardest chapter for most of you to read. Not because it is particularly detailed or complicated, but because it asks you to do something fundamentally and yet vitally important. Stand in front of the mirror and take a long, hard and honest look at yourself. Are you really and truthfully suited to the life of a bodyguard? Do you really look the part, and will others - both experienced BG teams and clients, really take you seriously? And then ask yourself, openly and honestly, do you really have the skills necessary to enter the industry?

THE BODYGUARDS LIFE

The life of a BG out on the road with a client is generally an insular and solitary life. It is not at all glamorous and, for a true professional, it is a hard and extremely stressful existence where the only priority is the person whom you have been tasked to protect. Forget about your girlfriend back at home, your wife and children, your mother's cancer or your grandfather's Alzheimer's, you have been tasked to protect someone in an environment that might possibly take his or her life and the consequences of this are enormous. This is the only priority you now have in your life; everything else is secondary and irrelevant. Sounds hard and callous? I told you I won't mince words, and I won't. It is a fact that, on a security and protection detail, nothing else matters to the professional BG other than the security and safety of his or her client. Every minute of every day his or her safety is paramount; there is room for nothing else. It is a fact that 99% of protection officers are not married and have no children, or were married and have since separated. On an operation there is no room for emotion. Once emotion creeps into the assignment then the BG is no longer able to perform his duties in an objective and unbiased fashion, he then becomes a liability to himself, his team and most importantly his client.

Most teams and individual operatives are at the beck and call of their clients 24 hours a day, seven days a week. It is therefore impossible for a professional operative to have other equally as demanding commitments. In order to be available at a moment's notice, operatives must have the ability and facility to just pack and go; they should either lead a single lifestyle or have a partner who doesn't care that they might not be home at the end of the day, or telephone for the next three months.

However, it is true to say most assignments are arranged and planned well in advance, and adequate notice is given, but there are occasionally assignments which are not and it is extremely unprofessional for an officer to have to turn down an assignment because he has not been given his usual three weeks notice. I can assure you, that officer definitely would not get called again.

This brings us to another factor - normal jobs. What job allows its staff to come and go as they please, taking time off at a moment's notice? Most BGs, when starting out, have to have other employment. It is virtually unheard of for a guard to step from a training course into a long term executive protection assignment. Most have to market and promote themselves and search hard for those first few contracts. But while they are doing that, what do they live on, how do they eat, buy cloths, buy equipment, and attend further training?

I have had CVs from hundreds of BGs who have other jobs. This is natural and perfectly normal, but what credibility does a BG have if his other job is an accountant, or a shop assistant, or a plumber? It just doesn't work. Can you imagine the conversation? "Yeh, I am a BG but when I am not working I stock shelves for B and Q". I have nothing against people who stock shelves for B and Q, but it just doesn't go with an international executive protection lifestyle. So if the newcomer has to have another job, he needs to have a job that has something to do with the security or related industry. Anything too diverse and different just does not hold any credibility with either his client or his team. The BG has to think what the client, the other team members or a security company will think. He needs to be convincing and stocking shelves at B and Q comes pretty low in the "convincing scale." The newcomer must look to the future.

CASE HISTORY

I had a six-week contract for a female BG in London. The pay was good, the work quite interesting but hard, demanding and long hours - looking after the wife of an Arab client is never an easy thing to do. I had just finished instructing on a beginner's six day training course and thought I would offer the contract to the only woman who attended the course. She had done extremely well. Prior to the course she had been working on the doors, and before that she was in the British Army for five or so years - so she had a good deal of related experience. She would also have been under the constant supervision from her team leader. It would have been a great start to her career and naturally I thought she would jump at the chance. She was to have an interview with the client Friday, with a view to start that Saturday morning. I called her, to which came her reply, "I'll go for the interview but won't be able to start work until the week after as I have a dinner date with my boyfriend - it is his birthday and I promised to take him out".

Needless to say I never called her again and I believe she is still on the doors and waiting for that first big break.

A FUNNY STORY

A few months ago, while I was back in the UK running a seminar for a few colleagues, I met someone in the industry who had just completed a very good two-week CP training course with a well-recognized military re-settlement training provider. He talked for what must have been well over an hour about his desire to enter the world of executive protection and how hard he is going to work and what an excellent BG he would be. Finally he asked me where I was based and I replied Moscow.
"F**k that", he said, "too bloody dangerous for me".
What about the other Former Soviet States?
"No", came his reply, "all too bloody dangerous!" I wondered just where he was prepared to work and then I laughingly imagined to myself a scenario with his client.
"Hi John, pack you bags, have to go to Bolivia to broker a big investment deal, need some security".

"Sorry Sir, bit too bloody dangerous for me".
"Errrr, then I might have to go to Moscow".
"Nope".
"What about Tanzania after Moscow?".
"All a bit too risky for my liking, but I'll take you to Bridport".

As a BG you will be required to provide security to those who need security, and in places where security is needed. If everywhere was as safe as Bridport, Dorset, none of us would have a job.

As a BG you should NEVER attempt to do anything that you have no experience of doing, but as a professional BG you may eventually have to go to some pretty inhospitable and dangerous places - and that is ultimately what being a BG is all about. Don't think about becoming a BG, if you are not prepared to become a BG.

DO I LOOK THE PART?

What does a BG look like? Of course, there are no rules and regulations as to what a BG should look like, but some people simply don't look anything remotely like a BG. It is a bit like the doors of nightclubs. Some people do look incredibly like a stereotypical doorman; big, hard looking, bodybuilder, shaven head, while others look totally out of place and completely out of their depth. I am not saying that he or she with the looks and physique of Mr Bean could not do the job, but looks matter in the world of the doors and they certainly matter in the world of executive protection. A BG must look self-confident; he or she must have an air of authority, a presence. They must be able to walk into a room and instantly command respect.

When marketing yourself it is vitally important to look at the way you are physically. A six-foot-two-inch, shaven-headed, 20-stone guy will probably never get asked to work in Bolivia protecting the Chairman of a multinational company. A five-foot-eight, average-built, average-looking ex Special Forces will probably never ever get asked to mind Mike Tyson. However if you are five-foot-eight, average-build, average-looking with no special skills or experience you will probably never get asked to protect anyone!

Many doormen go to the gym because they want to look like doormen, but there is nothing much you can do to look like a bodyguard. Either you do or you don't. Either you have a look and presence that others immediately notice, recognize and respect, or you don't. Every day, when walking down the street, I look at people passing me and can immediately see and feel if there is something more to them than just the way they look. Sadly, if you are one of those whom no one notices, whom everyone just walks past, there isn't much chance of getting noticed in the cut throat, tough world of executive protection.

DO I HAVE THE SKILLS?

Why do most prestige and highly paid protection contacts go to former members of the Special Forces or other specialized ex-military personnel? Quite simple, they have infinitely more skills and experience than the majority of civilians and as well as others from most other military regiments.

Before even thinking about embarking on a career as a BG, look at the skills you already have. If you don't have any other skills - hoping to learn everything you will ever need on a six to ten day training course, then either start studying hard and begin learning new and vitally important skills, or don't waste your time and money training.

If I was to employ a doorman for my nightclub, and two guys came for the job, both looking exactly the same and both passed the door supervisor's exam with the same high result, but one was a black belt in a variety of martial arts while the other had no martial art or self defence experience what-so-ever, who would I obviously employ? I would want to know that my door is secure, and the guy with the most experience would make me feel more secure than the guy with none.

The same applies to executive protection. Whenever a client looks at a CV, those who have other skills are those most likely to get the work. And this can especially be so if the client has an interest in the same things. I have known one BG to get a long-term contract based upon the fact that he was a competent horse rider, and the client loved to take out his horses every weekend. I have known a few BGs get contracts on board yachts and cruisers because they have their PADI scuba diving qualifications. And of course, many BGs get contracts because they speak two or three languages. It is a fact.

So ask yourself: are you really that dedicated and committed? Will you really spend time and money learning new skills, new skills relevant to this industry, or are you going to be lazy and hope for the best? Almost everyone will choose the second - I guarantee!

WHAT SKILLS?

So what skills are absolutely necessary before even embarking on a BG training course?

The first, and one of the most important, is to have strong self-defence skills. I don't mean Martial Arts. Martial Arts are fantastic as self-discipline, a sport, but unless the practitioner is particularly skilful, out on the streets the average martial artist is pretty ineffectual. I have personally seen three black belt martial artists floored by three devastating punches from an experienced street fighter. There are some excellent self defence and fighting styles that are fairly easy and quick to learn and which are particularly suited to the street: Krav Maga, Jiujutsu etc. If you are tasked to protect someone, you must be able to protect him or her - under any eventuality and in any environment. Without a good strong self-defence it would be impossible to defend yourself let alone someone else.

Most members of the Special Forces have devastating close quarter combat skills. Here in Moscow the Special Forces have a particularly brutal system that leaves no time for thoughts and feeling and in Moscow last year there were over 500 business style assassinations. In Russia, most bodyguards are ex Special Forces, as are most assassins, so the need to be skilled is paramount.

It is better to be well trained and never have to use the skills than to have no skill or training and jeopardize the safety of your client. Any CV that came to me which failed to show a good understanding of self-defence went straight in the dustbin. And believe me, there were hundreds. How can anyone, in their right mind profess to be a bodyguard and yet have no experience or skill at self-defence?

"Yeh, but I can handle myself", is a reply I hear time and time again when I question an applicant's lack of self-defence. "But I am not asking whether you can handle YOURSELF, I am asking whether you are skilled enough to quickly and effectively counter any possible violent attack on your client and evacuate him or her as quickly and as efficiently as possible using as much or as little force as necessary depending upon the environment and the conditions."

"Errr...?"

Handling yourself is irrelevant, effectively defending or successfully counter attacking requires experience and training. I have a colleague in Sweden who has worked protecting celebrities and artists throughout most of the ex Soviet States for the past ten years. Every single morning, without fail, he spends one hour in the gym with his training partner practising Krav Maga. He has done this almost every single day since he left the Croatian Special Forces ten years ago.

A second language is also very important. It is true that the international business language is English; however French, Spanish and German are also widely used. Most chairmen and directors of multi-national companies are extremely well educated, most speak two or three languages and, as their security adviser, it helps no-end if you can also speak another language. It is also infinitely easier to find work on the international arena if a BG has a second or third language, unless of course you just want to confine your work to Bridport. It isn't that difficult to learn another language, it is just that most people are lazy and simply cannot be bothered - they prefer to listen to the radio or turn on the TV to listening to language tapes and prastising their verb endings.

My Croatian friend obviously speaks Croatian, his native language. He lives in Sweden so speaks Swedish fluently. He also speaks English and German almost perfectly and basic Russian - as the CIS (ex Soviet States) has been where he has had most of his assignments.

Almost all of the British SAS have one other language apart from English and most also speak Arabic almost fluently. This is one reason why they get most of the well-paid Arab contracts. So ask yourself what language you speak apart from English? If you do not speak another language go out and buy a language course and start learning.

Occasionally I hear from men and women who have successfully completed a good training CP training course, who have a good self defence background and even have a second language, or actively learning one, but they don't have a driving licence!! It is true; some BGs are out there looking for work but can't drive. If you are one of those who can't legally drive, before you even think about this business get a driving licence and two or three years' driving experience. You will be ridiculed and even laughed at should a client ask you to drive his car but you tell him you can't drive. And you won't get insurance to drive executive vehicles without a few years' driving experience. While you are at it, it is also very good idea to get a motorcycle licence as well.

You will also need basic PC skills. Most reports are written using a PC; you must at least be able to do this as well as knowing a basic spreadsheet system for your accounts and a knowledge of the internet, e-mailing, sending and receiving confidential information etc.

Lastly, have you ever seen a fat BG? The BGs you see on newsreel, music awards, film premieres, films, do they look fat, unfit and out of shape? Do they smoke? Are they out of breath, sweating, struggling to keep up? Most professional BGs are very fit individuals and pay a great deal of care and attention to their appearance and health. Most train every day, both using weights and basic fitness, most are strong and have a good physique. A fat BG will not get work.

But, over the years, I have had many people sending in applications for my beginner's training courses being both overweight and unfit, almost all making vague promises to get fit and in shape once they pass the course. Why didn't they get in shape before going on a course? Because, as I have said many times already, most people are lazy and the vast majority of people have no real desire to do what it takes to become a professional BG.

CASE HISTORY

A 32-year-old friend decided when he was 26 that he wanted to become a BG. He had already served a few years in the parachute regiment, but had no real skills or qualifications pertaining to the civilian CP industry.

He got a job as a doorman at a local nightclub in Liverpool and spent the following four years developing his portfolio of skills and experience. He trained every day in a martial arts gym, he learnt French almost perfectly, took his HGV and motorcycle licence. He learnt to scuba dive and to ride a horse and he studied and read almost every book on the subject of executive protection. Every spare penny went towards the next course or learning a new skill; altogether he spent around 10,000 GBP on further training and development over the four-year period.

When he was 30 years old he got his first small contract for an English Lord and Lady. That contact swiftly led him to his second, for an elderly French aristocratic lady living in the Dordogne. Two years later he is still working for her, earning over 1000 pounds a week plus all his living expenses. He paid off his initial investment of 10k in just over two months and now has over 100 k sitting comfortably in his bank account. Maybe he was lucky, or maybe he worked damned hard.

Most people do not have the dedication and commitment of my friend, but those who do can certainly eventually reap the benefits and rewards. Someone once told me we are all responsible for our own destiny, and I believe that to be perfectly true. This brings us neatly onto training.

CHAPTER TWO

TRAINING COURSES

Fifteen years ago I attended a six-week training course and still, with every single day I work as a CPO, I learn something new. And I hope I will never stop learning. A BG training course is just one small step on a very long road, and should be treated as such.

It is important to note that, for those of you wishing to confine yourself to just working as a bodyguard within the UK, new laws affecting security consultants will be implemented in 2006. This will be covered in detail in the next chapter.

Many, if not most of you, will have already attended a BG training course. There are many good training providers, both in the UK and worldwide, and it is not the subject of this publication to detail who, in my opinion, is good or not. I have seen the first-rate and the appalling, and courses ranging from one day to a few weeks - all profess to offer recognized CP qualifications and diplomas. However, just to clarify things, there are currently NO *internationally* recognized qualifications within the civilian Close Protection arena. Every country and every company does its own thing, and offers training according to its specific environment and situation.

The training that I provide here in Moscow differs considerably to the training XYZ provides in the UK, which again is considerably different to training in the USA. But what is vitally important, before spending your hard earned money and giving up your valuable time, is to ascertain the credibility and legitimacy of the training providers.

You cannot hope to learn and discover what it is really like out in the field if the instructors themselves have no operational experience. It is imperative that the Instructors have a variety of international experience and in a variety of different environments. It is a complete waste of time and money if your instructors have only had experience "minding" a couple of celebrities once at a pop concert. Many instructors only instruct and have little or no real operational experience. Also, it is no good either if the instructors were bodyguards 15 years ago!!! A good instructor is an instructor with up to date operational experience.

It is vitally important that you confirm and verify the credentials of those instructing before signing up and paying for the course. Ask them lots and lots of questions, ask for real references and recommendations, not from their friends but from other students and, if possible, from employers. If they advertise they are ex-military instructors, ask to see their discharge papers. Everyone will show you their papers - even ex Special Forces. If they can't, don't or won't, don't waste you money.

There is one international training provider in the North East of England who refuses to be contacted by the telephone. E-mail is his only accepted method of communication. And yet time and time again students pay upwards of 2000 GBP for a course based on the references and recommendations that he provides. I asked him to provide me the contact details of those he lists as a reference. Of course he refused.

The owner of this company also professes to be an ex serving member of the SAS, which is also totally untrue. He was an ex-marine who trained with them once, about twenty years ago. The industry is full of people like this; some do offer excellent training but be cautious and make extensive inquiries and investigations.

Take a day off work and go to visit the companies that you are considering training with. The good and legitimate training providers will welcome you to their base or offices, offer you a coffee, chat to you and show you around. The others with something to hide won't want to know, they will refuse, citing a multitude of excuses and reasons. They just want you money.

I can give you a list of dozens of former ex-students of mine who have gone on to find work. Other good training providers should be able to do the same. Some of my ex students have been very successful, others haven't, but most of them will be more than happy to discuss their career with other hopefuls. Be wary if your training provider cites confidentiality as a reason for them not being able to give out names and contact details of their former students who are working in the field. It is an excuse; we are all in the same business and all should be able to freely contact and communicate with each other.

There is another training provider who, in their publicity and advertising, bestow a glamorous and international sounding name to their training camp. It gives you an impression of being a large and exclusive mansion somewhere in the country. However it is, in reality, the basement of the owner's end-terrace house. Sadly, by the time students have paid their fee, taken time off work and, quite possibly travelled hundreds if not thousands of miles to attend the course, there is not much they can do.

Don't rush into finding a suitable training provider - there is no hurry. Take you time and thoroughly research each and every company until you find the one most suitable for your requirements and career ambitions.

If you were going to buy a car for 2000 pounds you wouldn't just look from the road as you drive past and say - "yeh, that will do". Don't do the same with a training course - it could be the best decision you can make if you choose a good course and a complete and utter waste of time and money if you choose the wrong one. Sadly most people in this industry waste their money.

To have any credablity, a training course must be a minimum 6 - 10 days for a beginner's course, with another 6 - 10 days intermediate. There is no way that anything can be taught in any depth in less time. No employer would even consider your CV if the only training stated is a three day introduction. There is nothing in three days that would ever qualify someone to work as a BG. It takes one or two days just to be able to plan a good route report.

Courses should contain little or no keep fit - be highly suspect of courses that get you up at 5am every morning and beast you senseless until late in the evening. It is impossible to get anyone physically fit in a week or two, so why bother when there are other infinitely more important things to teach. Courses should be a mixture of practical and theoretical applications, with real life and relevant scenarios and situations. Courses should also give time for rest and recuperation, time for a personal review and reflection of the subjects covered with a facility to briefly go over again areas that, for some, were not clear the first time. You are paying a lot of money to be taught, so make sure you are taught.

Nothing can be learned if the student is so physically worn out that he or she can hardly stand, let alone listen to a two hour theoretical seminar on surveillance detection. Courses that end up making a student physically and mentally exhausted are a complete waste of time.

CASE HISTORY

An instructor once said to me that they push the students hard day in and day out simply to assess how they would operate in intensive and extremely violent situations. Excitedly I replied by asking what kind of course was it - for an elite SAS team with an assignment somewhere in deepest Bolivia? He laughed and looked at me as if I was an utter idiot. He informed me his course was for complete beginners - carpenters, doormen, an accountant, a paramedic. I replied by asking why then was he teaching students things that he knew they would never ever need and use. He replied by saying he could never sell the course for as much money as he did if he only detailed and taught what they would actually need to know during their first few years in the business.

A training course should be stressful and hard but not so hard it renders the student ineffectual and it should not use situations and scenarios that the student would never ever encounter. A beginner's course should just cover the basics; routes, surveillance, location reports, embussing and debussing, formations, basic road and driving procedures, car maintenance, first aid, and residential security. There is no need to teach more. A beginner's course that teaches IED, defensive and offensive driving, ECM sweeping, multi car convoys, and weapons is just glamorizing the industry in a way to entice you to part with your cash. There is no way a newly trained raw recruit will ever come across an IED in the course of his everyday assignments, nor will he ever need defensive and offensive driving skills and he will certainly never use a weapon. These subjects are all a complete waste of time for an apprentice. Stay clear of any course that offers these subjects to a complete beginner - they are just interested in your money.

There are many good training providers both in the UK and worldwide, but it is still a fact that training courses using Special Force or Military

Police instructors are the most highly regarded and respected. My colleagues in Moscow would not have heard of XYZ Training Company in Bridport, but they certainly have heard of the SAS and British Military Police. The SAS and the Military Police provide almost all of the high-risk close protection for government officials and diplomats worldwide. Therefore, as instructors, they would obviously have infinitely more experience than most other training providers. However, it is vitally important, as detailed earlier, to verify their status and that they are who they claim to be. There are many thousands of people who have actually done some form of training with the SAS, but it does not mean they have been members of the regiment. One ex-policeman boasted that he did indeed train with the SAS. What he actually meant was that he stood for 8 hours looking in the opposite direction while the SAS practised their aircraft hostage rescue techniques. He job was only to keep an eye for casual passers by!

There are also many people who claim to have worked closely with government organizations, police and Special Forces providing close protection for a visiting president or diplomat. What they really mean is that they stood at a barrier alongside a road for four hours until the convoy passed swiftly by.

Once you have completed a beginner's course and have a few small and extremely low risk assignments under you belt, then you can look at further developing your training portfolio. Or, if you have the time and money, attend a longer three / four week course where subjects can be covered in greater depth. There are also many good courses specializing in more specific subjects such as driving, IED, ECM, surveillance etc. The more courses and skills you have the easier it is to find work.

However, if you are six-foot-two, 22 stone, shaven-headed guy wishing to work solely within the celebrity market, it is of no real relevance taking a tactical SWAT course in Arizona or a kidnap and ransom negotiation course in El Salvador. You should select training more relevant and suitable to your chosen working environment. For the celebrity market training should be geared towards crowd control, restraint and holds, communication, surveillance, the law, the media, formation driving, first aid etc.

Any company that promises work as a BG after attending their course is lying but there are a few good security companies (mainly in the US) that spend a lot of money training their employees. There are also major employers, such as Vance International, that employ those who have attended their training, but even they do not promise work for everyone who attends their courses.

Without seeing every single applicant and assessing them over a matter of days, if not weeks, it is impossible for any company to promise anything. If a company does promise you a paid job at the end of training, ask them to pay for your course and then take the fee from your first wage packet. I can virtually guarantee they will all decline that offer.

CASE HISTORY

I do know of one training company in the UK that promises students work at the end of their course. A couple or so weeks after the course they call the student and tell them their first assignment is on but strongly suggest they work for free, just for the experience of their first real assignment. Most students, of course, say yes, anything to get their first real job. However, the job is naturally a set up - looking after the wife of the owner of the company for an afternoon while she wonders around the shopping Mall. But no one complains - most are too frightened of causing a stir and tarnishing their name before they even get started in the business.

Universities, colleges, night schools, correspondence courses - none can guarantee students work at the end of their studies and nor can a bodyguard training school. But you can choose the best university or college possible, or the most appropriate class at night school.

Shop around, research, make extensive inquiries and investigations and then, and only then, commit your time and money.

CHAPTER THREE

NEW UK LAWS

The Private Security Industry Act 2001 outlines a new system for the statutory regulation of the private security industry. The Act established the SIA (Security Industry Authority) whose aim is to improve the security industry's image so that the general public - and the wider business world - have a much clearer understanding of how the industry is regulated and who is entitled to work in it.

The SIA also wants to make the industry more attractive for employees - with better training opportunities, resulting in a recognised award, decent career progression and an improved and more professional working environment.

The SIA is the only authority in England and Wales dealing with these private security issues and they report directly to the Home Secretary.

The SIA's key functions are:

- to licence individuals in specific sectors and to approve security companies
- to keep under review the private security industry and the operation of the legislative framework
- to monitor the activities and effectiveness of those working in the industry
- to conduct inspections
- to set and approve standards of conduct, training and supervision within the industry, and
- to make recommendations to improve standards.

A key role for the SIA involves the managing and issuing of **licences** for people working in particular areas of the private security business.

How does this affect us, as Bodygaurds and Protection Specialists operating within the UK? Well, the SIA will issue licences to the following sectors of the security industry.

- security guarding
- door supervisors
- wheel-clamping
- private investigation
- security consultants
- keyholders

At present it does not specify Bodyguards and Close Protection Specialists as a separate heading, but it is currently assumed that Bodyguards will come under the umbrella of security consultants.

NEW LICENCES FOR SPECIFIC SECTORS

The SIA will issue licences to people working in different sectors of the security industry. The Act explains which sectors these are, although the Home Secretary can change the sectors as appropriate.

- The SIA will decide which skills you will need in order to hold a licence. These skills may vary according to the type of security work being carried out. The SIA will publish what the required skills are so people can check if they have them.

- If you need to apply for a licence you will have to show the SIA that you have the appropriate professional skills for the job. You will need to do this even if you have been working in the industry for a while. This means that you may need to do a short course of SIA-approved training.

- The SIA will keep a public register of everyone who holds a licence.

As the licensing programme rolls out in the prescribed sectors, SIA inspectors will have the right to enter certain types of premises such as security company offices and consultants' homes to check that consultants and staff hold valid licences. These inspectors will be working collaboratively with local authorities, the police and other agencies to ensure a co-ordinated approach to enforcement activity. The following categories of people will need licences:

- security contractors, directors of security companies and partners in security firms
- employees of security contractors, security companies and security firms
- agency workers performing the designated duties
- persons who manage or supervise security operatives supplied under contract by a security contractor (but not in-house supervisors of contractors)
- agency-supplied managers or supervisors of security operatives supplied under contract
- directors of security companies and partners in security firms who do not themselves carry out the designated activities
- in-house door supervisors and wheel-clampers and their employers, managers and supervisors
- others who wheel-clamp vehicles on private land against a release fee.

The Private Security Industry Act 2001 states that giving advice about security precautions in relation to a person or property or the acquisition of services involving a security operative is a licensable activity. So, if you set up a security company in the UK, you will soon need to be licenced. Even if you have a UK based company, but mainly operate abroad, you will still need to be licenced. The penalty for not having a licence and on conviction in a magistrates' court, is up to six months' imprisonment or a fine of up to 5,000GBP, or both.

GETTING A LICENCE

The SIA is expecting to begin licensing security consultants in 2006 with **NO** lead in period.

CRIMINALITY CHECKS

According to the SIA, criminal record checks will be robust and rigorous. In all cases an applicant's identity and criminal record check will be verified. Where the check reveals that the applicant has a record of convictions or cautions or warnings, they will consider these carefully on the basis of:

- How relevant the offences were to the licence applied for
- How serious the offences were, and
- How recent they were.

The SIA will pay special attention to offences involving violence, weapons, drugs, criminal damage and sexual offences. Anyone who has committed a relevant offence within two years immediately before their application will not get a licence. Anyone who has committed a serious offence within five years before the application is unlikely to be awarded a licence. While a licence is in force, the SIA will also receive updates of new convictions and cautions for licence holders and decide whether action needs to be taken on the continuation or revoking of the licence. The SIA will require access to at least a continuous five year period of verifiable, authoritative records against which to assess an applicant's criminal record. If the SIA can't obtain this (for example if an applicant has been overseas where verifiable records are unavailable) then it will **NOT** grant a licence.

TRAINING

We all know that the level of skills in the private security industry, including the close protection arena varies. In some areas training and qualifications have been developed, in others, including close protection and bodyguarding, little training and no qualifications exist. Standards of performance also vary because, up to the implementation of the Act, no attempt has been made to identify the skills needed across the industry as a whole.

The Security Industry Training Organisation (SITO) has developed modern apprenticeships for the major sectors of the security industry and a number of specific qualifications are available to employees and new entrants to the industry. However, this does not apply to all sectors and certainly not to the Close Protection sector. The aim of new training and qualifications is to increase the skills and professionalism of those employed in the industry and to raise standards of performance.

The SIA is defining standards of competence for licensing. The competency criteria for licensing will be based on a systematic analysis of skills, needs and trends, and on the identification of the knowledge required to perform the job to the required standard. The processes involved in the development of the standards of competency are:

- Looking at existing standards in the security industry and identifying any omissions
- Identifying the skills and knowledge required for specific jobs
- Looking at existing training and qualifications and identifying best practice
- Producing specifications for training and qualifications for each security industry sector
- Talking with each industry sector to develop training modules and new qualifications

From here, the SIA will specify new qualifications within the security consultancy arena that will build on those that currently exist and include best practice in training. In developing the new qualifications the SIA will take into account the changing roles of those already employed in the industry and the requirements for new skills and knowledge. The SIA will not be developing training courses or qualifications. Instead, in conjunction with the qualification regulation authorities, it will endorse awarding bodies to deliver the new qualifications. The SIA will recognise certain, relevant existing qualifications or parts of a qualification, including those from overseas. Existing qualifications will be looked at to see if they meet the new requirements allowing the holder exemption from the new training requirements. The SIA will encourage recognition of qualification achievements where possible but this can only be on the basis of careful evaluations of such awards on a case-by-case approach.

COMPETENCY POLICY

Working with the security industry, the Qualifications Curriculum Authority and awarding bodies, the SIA has developed a competency strategy in support of licensing. This will set out the standards of competencies needed by individuals employed within the private security industry. The SIA will recognise existing qualifications where these meet requirements. Where gaps exist, new qualifications will be developed. The SIA is working with the Qualifications and Curriculum Authority who will accredit the qualifications and the Learning and Skills Council who may provide appropriate funding to offset the costs of the training.

The competencies needed to obtain a licence and begin working in the private security industry and the training courses to achieve them are likely to be made up of units. These may include first aid, health and safety communications, conflict management, knowledge of relevant legislation, etc.

THE BENEFITS

- A training and qualifications framework leading to licensing which meets the needs of the private security industry and is based on best practice.
- Increased skills and competence of those working within the industry raising standards.
- Employees within the private security industry will see for the first time a clear career path through the industry from the moment they join.
- The security industry will be more attractive to potential employees and will have a better public image.

Competencies will be tailored to meet the needs of each industry sector and will give new entrants the skills and knowledge to do their job. At the end of training, people will need to sit a short exam and if successful will get a qualification. This qualification will be needed in order to get an SIA licence. Therefore, everyone joining in the private security industry will be trained and qualified for their role before they start work. This will lead to a more competent and professional workforce.

COST OF A LICENCE

The cost of the licence application will be 190 GBP. This will cover the licence holder for a three year period. Individuals will have to incur the cost of the licence fee but if you are working for a security company your employer may provide funds for the licence if they wish to do so.

> *Note: The application fee covers the cost of processing the application and is chargeable regardless of the decision that is reached at the end of the process. You will NOT get a refund should your application be rejected - so find out first whether you fulfil all the criteria required for licensing.*

Security Consultants and CPOs cannot make applications yet as the systems and processes are not yet in place and the criteria has not been fully finalized. If you want to be updated then join the Worldwide Federation of Bodyguards (E-mail: TheWFB@aol.com) and they will keep you fully updated. Or log onto www.The-SIA.org.uk

CHAPTER FOUR

YOUR CV

So, you have taken a long hard look at yourself and decided that you are indeed exactly suited to the BG industry and you have no ties and commitments, which may hinder your progress. You have a good solid background in self-defence; you are learning second language and can now drive both a car and a motorcycle. You are fit and healthy and have attended and passed with flying colours a 15 day CP training course. Now what do you need to do?

Firstly you need a CV, or profile. Having a great product is wonderful but completely useless if no one knows about it. So you must now market yourself. You must now tell as many people as possible that you are here and you are the best and most conscientious bodyguard in the business.

I have seen hundreds if not thousands of CVs. Most, I am afraid, go in the bin. It isn't that I don't appreciate the time and effort some people have made putting their CV together, or the cost, but if it doesn't conform to my expectations, and if it doesn't fall on my doormat at exactly the right time, I will have no need for it and sadly it will go straight in the dustbin. If I had kept every CV I have received over the past 15 years I would have no room in my apartment for anything else.

In this chapter I want to discuss what a proper, professional and well presented CV should look like, and what will make me stop and look at one but discard another. However, this is just a personal view; other people in other companies may have other different opinions.

I am busy. I simply do not have the time to go through everything that comes through my letter box. Sometimes I have over 20 letters a day so I must quickly and effectively discard immediately those which I consider worthless or uninteresting. I am no different to anyone else; almost every other security manager in almost every other company does exactly the same as me. Fact.

Firstly, your CV should be no longer than two A4 pages. I have seen CVs with over 15 pages; with colour copies of every single certificate imaginable, some even going back to high school. If I want to call someone in for an interview, I will request to see his or her certificates then, but not before.

The front page should contain your full name, a mailing address, a landline telephone number, a mobile number and an e-mail address. Everyone in this business needs an e-mail address. If you haven't got one then go to your nearest internet cafe or public library, go online, go to hotmail or yahoo, or any of the other hundreds of servers and get an e-mail address. It is such a simple thing to do.

Some CVs don't list a landline number. There should always be a landline number listed - any CV that lists only a mobile telephone number is again immediately discarded. It costs next to nothing to have a second dedicated landline installed in most properties - and there is no reason why a land line telephone number cannot be listed on a CV. You would be suspicious if a security company only operated from a mobile number - the same applies to individuals.

Also, when trying to contact a mobile number, it is frequently switched off. Guess what? I never call again. If I cannot get hold of someone when I want to, or if there is no answer machine, I will not try again. Unless the CV is something really special, it will go in the bin. I will have another three or four good CVs sitting in front of me.

If there is an answer machine, I will of course leave a message. I understand people work, drive cars, and live in areas of poor reception. But if my message is not replied to within 24 hours, again that CV gets discarded. A BG should be available 24 hours a day, 7 days a week - their mobile should be switched on beside their bed at night and next to them when they have a sh*t in the morning. A professional bodyguard should be available at any time, even on holiday.

If I am abroad I will frequently use e-mail to contact someone. However, many times I won't actually receive a reply for days and days. E-mails should be checked each and every day, preferable twice, in the morning and at night. In Moscow we are three hours ahead of the UK, so my office day will finish at about 10pm - 7pm UK time. If I finished work at 7pm Moscow time I might miss any important messages coming in after 4 pm UK time. You are now an international BG - so think about the international arena and be available 24/7.

And think carefully about your e-mail address. I have seen all sorts of stupid e-mail addresses listed on CVs. Can you imagine the security manager at BP e-mailing BrainDeadMoron@hotmail.com? Your e-mail address should be simple, fairly conservative, easy to remember and not a muddle of letters and numbers or stupid phrases and words.

CVs that don't have a postal mailing address also go in the bin. I have to ask why they don't have a mailing address? Are they homeless and living on the streets? I perfectly understand that most people wouldn't want to list their home address, but a Box Number can be rented from the Post Office for about 60 GBP a year. There are also many other office services that offer postal addresses for a reasonable yearly fee. Mail Boxes Etc offer an address available 24/7 for about 200 GBP per year. If an individual cannot afford 200 GBP a year then he or she should find another job and save hard for a few months. It is better to wait and present yourself properly and professionally than to rush and do things incorrectly and unprofessionally. It is hard to develop a good reputation, but so easy to get a bad one.

I even had a CV sent to me about a year ago that had his name listed in bold at the top of the paper, and under contact details "See web site"! Needless to say, that also went in the bin.

I get lots of CVs with photos, either attached or scanned onto the page. Sometimes it is good to send a photo, other times it can have drastic consequences. Can you imagine a conservative elderly female aristocratic client receiving a photo of a 22 stone shaven headed man with a broken nose? If you do want to send a photo, then attach only a passport size photo and dress in a suit and tie. I have seen photos of applicants in tee-shirts, jeans and even a gym vest. Personally, however, I would prefer not to receive photos. If I like the look of a CV I would ask for more info, and then a photo just prior to interview, but rarely before. Full-length doorman type photos are a complete no-no, as are photos in anything but a suit and tie. Baring in mind that almost every single unsolicited CV gets binned, money spent getting hundreds of photos developed, or the ink of a printer, is generally wasted. Invest money, but don't waste it!

Under your address and contact details you should next list you military service (if appropriate), giving regiment and time served, as well as any overseas posting and active service. It is a fact that those with a military background will often find it much easier to get work, and it is even easier still for those seeing actual active service in a conflict. After my time in Bosnia during the war I was offered many other Military style contracts that would never have been offered to me had I not seen conflict.

Those who have served in the recent Iraqi conflict will stand an infinitely better chance of getting a job than Mr Carpenter. However, it certainly does not mean that there isn't work for Mr Carpenter, it can just take a little longer and can be harder to find.

Nevertheless there are many clients out there who prefer not to employ those from a military background. I know many very good civilian operatives working with celebrities and businessmen worldwide.

CASE HISTORY

From a civilian background, Steve attended one of my training courses in Wales. He had a door company that provided doormen and stewards to numerous nightclubs and bars in his home town. After the course he went back to the doors, studied hard and invested in further more specialized training with my colleague in Sweden. Since his initial training four years ago, Steve has worked with celebrities including Tim Robbins, Susan Sarandon, and Shaun Penn and has travelled to Gaza, Kosovo and Brazil.

It is not important to mention what school you went to, or what GCSE qualifications you have; it is irrelevant, but your military service isn't and is important.

Under your military service list your CP training and training courses - the length of each course, where it was held and with which training company. However do not list 26 different subjects studied on a beginner's six-day course. Employers will immediately know it would be impossible.

Also list other specialized training courses - again what, where, how long and with whom. List the company and their contact details, so your status can be verified. I would not dream of employing anyone whom I hadn't vetted and verified. And nor would any other employer.

If you have already completed close protection assignments then list these after your courses and training. Do not list anything you haven't done, or anything your employer refuses to sanction. Only list those assignments you have authorization and approval to list. It destroys your credibility if you list an operation protecting a chairman of a multinational corporation in Uzbekistan but, when I call to ask for further details, you say, "Sorry, top secret, can't give details". And don't bullsh*t either; don't say you've done something that you haven't, you soon get found out.

For every job that you do as a BG you should have a full report associated with it. If you don't have a report of every assignment you have completed you are not professional and I will not employ you. Simple.

CASE HISTORY

I had a CV from a BG who claimed to have worked in the oil fields of Moscow. Normally I would throw such crap immediately in the bin, but on this occasion I couldn't resist calling him. The few pounds I would spend on the call would be well worth the entertainment. Not knowing I was calling from Moscow, he enthusiastically started to tell me about a job he did. After a couple of minutes I interrupted him, told him I was actually based here in Moscow and the nearest oilfields were in fact thousands of kilometers south in the Caspian Sea. There was a moment's silence and he hung up.

Another time I met a so-called female bodyguard in Manchester who professed to speak fluent Russian - she said she had worked as a translator for Army intelligence. When I said a few simple words to her in Russian she went red with embarrassment and told me she had forgotten most of her Russian.

If you bullsh*t you soon get found out. Tell it as it is or don't tell it at all.

Under operations you should then list anything else that is relevant to the industry. List the other qualifications and skills you have, what languages you speak and what martial arts you have studied. Be truthful, it is better to be honest than to be dishonest and get found out. Don't list that you like reading Shakespeare aloud while looking after your neighbour's collection of homing pigeons. You are not applying for a normal 9 - 5 job, so just put only that which is relevant to security.

Your CV should be printed on good quality paper - not on normal cheap white photocopy paper. Laid or woven, 100 gsm is the best and looks the business. It has to appear interesting and professional. The lettering should be printed without errors and faults, properly typeset in black ink and obviously all words should be spelled correctly. There is no excuse for a poorly prepared CV.

Also, bear in mind, most CVs sent via e-mail are never even opened let alone read. I never open any file from an unknown sender. Anything that I am not expecting gets deleted. It is easy to delete an e-mail, but almost everyone opens up their normal mail.

CVs should not be folded into a DL envelope but sent in an A4 envelope. It should also be properly stamped. Many times I have had to pay for excess postage, and then of course once opened it goes straight into the dustbin. If someone can't be bothered to put on the proper postage then I certainly cannot be bothered to read it.

Along with your CV, send your business card. Everyone should have a business card - it is a sign of professionalism. Out of twelve guys who attended a small seminar I gave a few weeks back in the UK, only three gave me their business card. Attach your business card with a paper clip to the top left hand corner of your CV, over the staple that holds the two sheets together. Your business card should be printed in the same fonts as your CV.

Your CV is your gateway to an introduction and perhaps employment. Your CV should reflect your professionalism and attitude. Spend time getting it right, and update it frequently as your skills, experience and portfolio of operations develop.

THE INTERVIEW

So, you have finally managed to get yourself an interview with either the client, a representative of the client, the security manager or a security company. Now what? No matter how tough or hard he is, no matter what previous experiences he has had, almost everyone is nervous going to his or her first ever interview for a position in executive protection. I have seen the hardiest of men crumble at the thought of sitting suited and booted in front of a panel and answering question upon question. Without doubt, interviews can be tough, especially the first when you have to persuade a prospective employer that, although you have had no real CP experience, you are the one, above all others, who is best suited to that specific position. The key to a successful interview is to prepare. Take time out to investigate the company, know who the directors are, what contracts they have, who they protect. Find out about the client, any incidents that have happened, what plans they have for the future. The more information you have on the client the more you will impress those interviewing you.

CASE HISTORY

A colleague went for an interview with a shipping company that was planning to ship a cargo of high value machinery from Sweden to St Petersburg, and then by boat all the way through Russia down to the oil fields in the Caspian Sea. Their requirement was for a Western European Leader and, naturally, a team of fully armed Russian guards to escort the boat to its final destination. It was a two-month contract, high risk, and high profile. He got the job because he had taken a lot of time and care planning his interview. He had maps of the route, he found out about specific areas of Russia along the route that might be subject to bandits and hijackers, he knew about the company and their presence in the Caspian Sea, he even remembered the names of the President and Company Directors. His wages, as well as a small commission on the Russian guards he hired made him almost 1000 USD per day!!!

Most first interviews will be with a representative of the client or his or her security manager. If you pass that stage you may then be called to meet the client. Protecting celebrities is different to protecting executives. In the corporate world you will almost always be interviewed by the client however in the celebrity world, unless you were tasked to be up close, it is rare you would meet the client until the operation.

Remember, you are there to provide your client with security and protection. When being interviewed your physical presence is the most important element you have. As I mentioned in Chapter 1, do you really have what it takes? He will be hiring you as a bodyguard to protect himself and quite possibly his wife and children. Can he trust you with the lives of his family? This is an extremely important thing to think about. Maybe you look in the mirror and say, "of course he can", but will he? If, after meeting you, do you project the qualities that give surety to your client that he will be safe?

How you dress is very important. Will your client feel you have the right "look."? When you dine with him in a Four Star Restaurant, or check into some of the most expensive hotels in the world, will you embarrass him by the way you appear. In the corporate world looks are vitally important - in the celebrity world looks are important but in a completely different way. A celebrity looking for security might possibly be very impressed with the appearance of a 22 stone, shaven head, tough looking man, but not in the corporate world.

Do not be too pushy. Don't talk too much, answer concisely and honestly and know what you are talking about. If this is your first, third or tenth interview, you client will still probably know a lot more about security than you do, if you lie or bullsh*t you will certainly get found out. Impress him or her with your humility, with your sincerity and with your knowledge of the industry, and not with the fact you can shoot a moving target at 100 yards and break someone's neck in a mili-second.

Let your very presence speak for itself. The truly "tough" don't have to prove it. The great martial artists do not have to explain how many belts they have. Be recognized and respected by your confidence and manner. Don't blow your own trumpet; it may have worked for Achilles in the Odyssey but it won't work for you.

Make sure you take your portfolio to each and every interview you attend. Your portfolio is your personal history of everything relevant and pertaining to executive protection. It should contain your certificates and awards from the military, the police, martial arts schools, gun schools, bodyguard schools as well as military discharge papers, firearms licences, bodyguard licences, references, a few copies of your CV, your business cards, blank letterheads, a full length and a passport photo and copies of your passport and any driver's licences you hold. If your client is interested, he'll inspect them.

You don't have to show an employer the .44 Magnum you carry in a shoulder holster. If he asks you if you are licensed to carry a concealed weapon, a simple "yes" will do. Let your confidence and worth show in every word, every gesture and movement you make. Impress him, but subtly. Remember - your first contact with your client should end with him or her having a pleasant feel about you and a sense of quiet ability. He will, without doubt, be interviewing others, let them brag and boast and bullsh*t. It is not what you are about, nor is it what this industry is about, and your client will know this only too well. Even if he likes you it is doubtful he will make an immediate decision.

Even if you don't get the first job you apply for, or the second, learn from each interview and keep applying. If you walked down the street asking everyone for 10 pence, you will sure to be given 10 pence at some point. Take this philosophy with you to your interviews. For every "no" you are one step closer to a "yes" - unless of course you really do not have what it takes !!!!!

The next few pages detail a typical CV. Well organised, precise and to-the-point, it details Military Service, Training, Courses and Work Experience as well as full contact details (deleted for publication purposes). It gives a good overall impression of the applicant.

Example of a Good CV

Name: *****
Address: *****
Tel: *****
Fax: *****
Mobile: *****
E-mail: *****

PERSONAL ATTRIBUTES

A well presented individual who thrives on responsibility and is able to communicate across all levels. Fully able to command respect of superiors and colleagues alike with an exceptional aptitude for exceeding all expectations whilst working as a member of any team. Possessing a strong ability to carry out tasks within a defined framework or whilst working under own initiative. Able to provide premium levels of commitment and enthusiasm within any work situation demanding responsibility, reliability and trustworthiness.

WORK HISTORY

ROYAL ARMOURED CORPS ~ VARIOUS LOCATIONS HOME & ABROAD. 1989 - 1996.

Full Crewman - Challenger Main Battle Tank (4 years)
　　　　　　Close recon (4 years)

- Driver - Loader - Gunner
- Trained weapons - 9mm to 120mm
- Assistant Instructor in Nuclear, Biological and Chemical Warfare
- Staff Car Driver - Grade B & A at Army School of Mechanical Transport, Hull.
- Offensive and Defensive Driving.
- Detailed Route Planning.
- Suspect Devices Search.
- Personal Security.
- Team Medic Course with Security Operations and Training Advisory Team, Sennelager.
- Search Team Member - Suspect Vehicles, Northern Ireland.
- Fighting in Built-up Areas Course, Sennelager.
- Team member of four responsible for training drivers on the use of SNATCH armoured Landrovers and cars whilst on NI tour.

- Member of Officer Commanding (Major Richard Parry) protection team.
- Various guard duties ranging from mobile and foot patrols, incident logging, CCTV monitoring, issue of keys etc., visiting personnel close contact escort duties whilst on camp.
- Trained Signal Team Member - VHF and UHF (bid 2000 secure speech).

Attachments - Detachments and Postings

- Joint Arms Control Investigating Group May - August 1991.
- Escorting Russian Officers within UK - NATO Agreement of Weapons Disposal.
- Operation Granby 1990 - 1991.
- 16/5th Queens Royal Lancers to train newly deployed soldiers and work in tandem with "A" Squadron in desert warfare
- Maze Prison, Northern Ireland. October 1993 - January 1994.

Regimental Internal Course (14 Intelligence Corps Based)

- Exit of vehicles under fire.
- Return of fire from both static and moving vehicles.
- Tactical driving to evade possible threats.
- Recognition of threats.
- 9mm pistol range work
- First Aid Instructor Life Saver and Life Saver Plus.
- Personal Driver. Brigadier J.D.P.E. Ferguson O.B.E Deputy Chief of Staff. 1993 - 1994.
- Signal/Driver Rebroadcast Station.

Decorations

- Gulf, with Clasp.
- GSM, with Clasp.
- Kuwaiti Liberation medal.
- Saudi Star.

SNOWDONIA SURVIVAL SCHOOL
NORTH WALES - 1996 - 2001.
Instructor

6TH CADET BATTALION ROYAL WELCH FUSILIERS
NORTH WALES - 1997 - 2001.
Instructor

FORTESQUE'S TOTAL EVENT MANAGEMENT
LONDON - 2002 - 2003.
Team Member

VERIFIED SECURITY
LONDON - MARCH 2003 - JUNE 2003.
Residential Security Team Member
- Vice President of Premiership Football Club.

CANNON SECURITY
LONDON - JULY 2003 - CURRENT.
Close Protection Team Member
- Senior member Royal Family United Arab Emirates.

FOUNDATION EDUCATION
YSGOL ABERCONWY
NORTH WALES. 1983 - 1988.
G.C.S.E. Level
- Mathematics and Welsh

PERSONAL DETAILS

Date of Birth: 19 November 1971. Single.
- Full Clean Driving Licence.
- Class II
- Track
- Fork-Lift
- PSV
- Hazmat - Licensed to carry all explosives, solid/liquid fuel, gas and oils.

INTERESTS
- All aspects of computing including hosting and supporting MSN chatrooms.
- Rugby.
- Skiing.

REFERENCES
- TD Roberts. RSM Royal Welch Fusiliers Bethesda, North Wales.
- Colin Rigby. Snowdonia Survival School, North Wales.
- References from the above and current and previous employers will be obtainable upon request.

CHAPTER FIVE

STARTING YOUR OWN COMPANY

An important fact to remember - **MOST SECURITY COMPANIES EMPLOY INDIVIDUALS AND MOST SECURITY CONTRACTS ARE AWARDED TO SECURITY COMPANIES**. So you have to decide whether you want to work as an individual for a security company, or set up your own company and work directly for a client. Because of the nature of the business, most clients like to be invoiced from a legitimate security company, rather than put individual BGs on their pay roll - even if the security company only employs one or two people - the owner and his / her partner, invoicing is still preferable to PAYE.

YOUR COMPANY

Your company should be Limited and VAT registered. VAT registration means that the annual turnover is above 55 thousand pounds a year. A security company with a turnover of less than 55k is barely trading and most clients will not deal with a company that financially insecure. Being VAT registered certainly does not guarantee financial stability but at least it gives that impression. A Limited company can be bought for about 90 GBP, and can be registered in less than a week. There are many companies whose sole purpose is to set up and sell Limited companies and most also offer mail addresses and telephone answer services as well. I have personally used Midland Company Formations in Birmingham on a couple of occasions.

It is vitally important to carefully choose the name of your company as well as its corporate identity. It is unlikely that British Petroleum would employ the services of a company called "Hard Man Protection Services". They would prefer a more corporate and subtle image. However a night club, boxing match, film premiere, concert and maybe some celebrities might use such a company. But it is a fact that most clients actually do not like to see the words Bodyguard, Protection, Executive, Magnum etc. They are too obvious for most corporations and employers.

If you introduce yourself as either "Magnum High Risk Bodyguard Protection" or "Global Response" I can almost guarantee that "Global Response" would win most attention. Look at the names of many of the major players in the industry and decide for yourself: Control Risks, Drum Resources, Vance International, Grant Vymple, DSL, Music and Arts, Saladin.

BROCHURES AND CORPORATE MARKETING

Your brochure should be specific to the services you provide, and be of a good quality. Good quality brochures are rarely thrown away. If you supply 20 stone, shaven head doormen then show 20 stone, shaven head doormen, but if you want to market to the international corporate arena then the brochure should be as subtle and unassuming as your company name. It should not contain pictures of black-suited sunglasses standing awkwardly around a car - most of the corporate and celebrity world actually detest this dreadful image. You don't have to show any obvious bodyguard-type images. Try to be inventive yet subtle, take a look at Group 4's or The Armour Group's corporate brochure, both excellent quality and the images used highlight the text without giving clues as to the services provided.

Your brochure must have the company's full contact details, as well as all company information including its registered office address and company registration number. The images must be of good quality and pin sharp, and make sure you have permission if you use someone else's images. They could be copyrighted and you don't want your new company to be the subject of a lawsuit. Text must also be expertly written.

Some new businesses think it is better to offer multiple services on one brochure hoping to cover any eventuality. I personally think this is a mistake. There are only a few individuals skilled at any more than a couple of specialities and I think it is infinitely better to be known for providing a few services expertly than many services poorly. SPS in Hong Kong provide an expert Kidnap and Ransom consultancy service and little else - they are known worldwide for their speciality and work for many of the major insurance institutions. If you ask them for a service they don't provide, they will politely decline and suggest you contact an associate who is skilled in that specific area. If you are a black, female bodyguard who specializes in providing protection to black female celebrities, then market yourself accordingly. There are hundreds and hundreds of companies providing general security services but far fewer specializing.

WEB SITE

In this day and age I certainly believe it is extremely important to have a company or individual web site - and most sites are now extremely cheap to set up and host. Anet (www.sitewiz.co.uk) will design (basic, but acceptable) and host a five-page site for around 150 GBP for one year. There is no reason why most companies cannot have a basic web site. I use the internet extensively and have contacted security companies in the most unusual places, in the most obscure countries. It would have been virtually impossible without it.

However a web site should be used as an information tool only, and should not be a substitute for hard copy marketing. I get much e-mail from companies inviting me to look at their web site, unfortunately 99% of these e-mails I have to delete. Generally I don't have the time to look through every web site that arrives in my inbox, and when I do have the time - on the Metro, sitting in a cafe - I then don't have internet access. It is good to have a web site, but only as an extra and not as the main method of marketing and promoting.

Web sites should upload quickly and be concise and informative. Living in Moscow, where internet access can sometimes still be slow, there is nothing worse than sitting waiting for a site to upload. If it takes too long, I press "close" and look at the next site. A web site with too many pages or with one extremely long page is also not a good idea. A home page, a contacts page and three or four other pages is just about the right size.

Lastly, there is nothing worse than having to fill out an inquiry form online, never ever have a reply form attached to your web site, have an e-mail link only, and again make sure e-mails are checked daily.

CHAPTER SIX

HOW TO GET WORK

In this chapter I want to detail a few tips and advice for getting work. If getting work as a BG was easy no one would ever be unemployed, and everyone would be busy protecting clients around the world and certainly not reading this manual. Your imagination and resilience is the only limiting factor in your search for work. I can guarantee that most of you will remain seated on your backside and not take on board one suggestion or tip in this manual, and yet you will still complain and moan about the business and bitch at those who are working and wonder why you are not. I know because I have seen it time and time again.

CASE HISTORY

Remember Steve, who is protecting major international celebrities and has travelled to some extremely interesting and remote places? He came on my training course with a close friend of his, Pete. They were working the doors together. They both trained hard, both passed the course and were both generally good guys. However, Steve has had quite a bit of success but Pete, almost none.

Steve and Pete did their first assignment together, along side five other novices. Steve and the others knuckled down and worked hard, but Pete moaned about everything, his living conditions, the food he ate and the wages. After their first assignment Steve sent out thousands of letters, made hundreds of telephone calls and went to visit company upon company. He was inventive and contacted festival organizers, witness protection schemes, film producers, journalists, authors, and entertainment agencies. In fact anyone who might be remotely interested in the services he could provide.

Pete did little. He called me and asked why he had no success. I asked him what he had done so far - he said he had sent out about 200 letters. I think that he genuinely believe that spending 50 GBP sending a few hundred letters would get him that elusive and well paid contract. Needless to say, he is still on the doors.

Finding work will certainly not be easy - and don't forget, there are thousands of other BGs doing exactly the same. You have to work hard, be consistent and never give up.

By taking on board the suggestions made so far, getting work might be a little easier, but it is still incredibly hard to get those first few assignments. Starting in this industry is a Catch 22 - no one will employ you if you have no experience and you can't get experience without that first job.

So what steps can you take to get on that first rung of the ladder?

The first and the most important thing is to spend time networking. Develop as many contacts as you possibly can within the industry. Be polite, be professional, don't bullsh*t and don't get caught up in politics.

If you become known as a bullsh*tter, then you will have no chance of ever securing work. The industry is small and people talk. Tell the truth and remain humble, people will respect you a lot more and may eventually give you that first break. Don't get involved with any negative feeling and the resentment of others not working - do what you believe is right for you and your business and stick with it - regardless of what others are doing or saying.

Keep positive and never give up. It is a fact that most businesses fail during their first few years because the owners simply give up. Hopefully you have another job so in theory you have nothing to loose. It can take one year or ten years to get that first contract but while you are earning, and thus investing in the development of your portfolio of skills and experience, you are not loosing anything, apart from your time.

SUGGESTIONS FOR FINDING WORK - THE CELEBRITY MARKET

You have decided that your speciality lies within the celebrity market, and that you want to provide security to singers, artists, actors, pop stars etc but you don't know where to start. Apart from hoping to bump into them one evening at your local - there is virtually no chance of getting even remotely close to any celebrity. They tend to keep themselves to themselves and well away from public places. Also there is little point in sending them mail, it is extremely rare for any celebrity to open and read his or her own mail - they have secretaries, agents and managers that do that kind of work, as well as the hiring and firing. So here are a few tips.

TIP 1

The publication Showcase is the bible within the entertainment agency industry. It costs about 40 GBP and lists celebrities, their managers, agents and record companies. So, for instance, you want to contact Madonna. First you look up her name in the index. Under her name is listed her manager, her UK agent and her record company. You then go back to the index and look up their contact details. Another book is called The Red Book; it is roughly the same and provides the same service. Both are available from any good book shop or online. You can also list your company in Showcase - a basic listing is free.

You can, of course, send hundreds upon hundreds of brochures or CVs to every agent, record company and manager listed, but almost all will be binned. The best and most efficient way is to telephone first asking if you can send them your details. Most will say no. Thank them politely and remember to call again a few months later. A few, however, will say OK, even reluctantly, but the most important thing is to get the name of the person for whose attention you should mark your details. Now you have a name and you can use that name time and time again.

Send them your information, addressed specifically to the person concerned, and a covering letter mentioning your call. You must follow this up with another call about a week later, politely asking if the information you sent has been received and whether they have had time to review it. If they say they have no need for your services, thank them politely and promise to call again in the future - which you will of course do. You have now started to develop an acquaintance which might one day prove profitable.

TIP 2

Subscribe to all the entertainment magazines and newspapers: e.g. The Stage and Television Today, Empire, NME, Music Week, Classical Music, Jazz Journal, Top of The Pops Magazine, Mojo etc. A full list can be seen in the Willings Media Guide. Every month see who is performing and where. Then contact the agent, promoter or manager asking if they require extra security / chauffeurs / stewards etc for his or her concert in Bridport on the 26th July. Most will say no, but again a relationship is being developed and you are starting to effectively network. If they say no, ask to send them your company brochure just in case!! Also look at who is visiting the UK and who is releasing new records (promotional tours normally follow new releases).

TIP 3

Buy The Events and Festival Directory and write to each and every festival organizer asking to tender for their next music festival. You will need to write well in advance, as most tenders are awarded at least three months prior to the event, but it is also worth contacting organizers a lot nearer the time asking if they have adequate provision and again whether you can post them your brochure.

TIP 4

Contact smaller record companies with up and coming yet little known bands and singers. Ask if you can work for them at their concerts for free or for the price of a meal. It is good experience and gets you in at the start of the band's career. You may not make much money initially, but, if they eventually make the big time, you will be with them forever thereafter.

TIP 5

Subscribe to Hollywood magazine and find out the schedule of international location film shoots. There are hundreds of films shot in England each and every year. Hollywood magazine gives contact details of the producer, director, dates and location as well as contact details of the organizers. Contact them and offer your services when they come to the UK.

TIP 6

Read the tabloids every day - when you read that a pop star or celebrity has had problems with the paparazzi, stalkers, drunken yobs etc, write to their manager (whom you have found in Showcase) and offer your services, detailing the account in question and how you feel able to assist in the future.

Eventually something will work and you will be given your first break. Then work the hardest you have ever worked, be as professional as you could ever be, providing more than is asked for, don't moan and groan or complain and you can only go forward.

SUGGESTIONS FOR FINDING WORK - THE CORPORATE MARKET

If pop stars really aren't your cup of tea and if you don't like the celebrity lifestyle - the late night parties, the groupies, the waiting in the foyer until your client wakes from his drug fuelled drunken concert the night before - then you might prefer the regimented lifestyle of the corporate sector, with the business meetings, expensive lunches, the shopping trips and school runs, flights in the private jet and executive class luxury.

Both sound appealing, in their own way, but the demands of protecting the businessman are very different from that of the celebrity sector and require a totally different approach.

It has to be said, there is little work for personal protection within the corporate sector based in the UK. Thankfully we still live in a relatively secure and safe environment, where the executive can still drive his or her Bentley around the country roads without any risk of assassination or kidnapping - something that would certainly be impossible here in Russia as well as in many other countries worldwide. In the UK, if a criminal attempt or threat is made on an executive's life, the police usually step in and provide security and protection without the need for private companies.

However, most top executives employ a chauffeur whose job tends to occasionally overlap into security. There is lots of work for security chauffeurs; the best place to start is to attend a 5 day chauffeur course run by the British Chauffeurs Guild in London. With their diploma, a job can almost certainly be guaranteed.

Apart from the corporate sector, there are other opportunities to provide UK based personal protection. The Arabs almost always employ security and protection, as do arms and diamond dealers, executives transporting valuable documents, stock, money etc.

Although most of the corporate sector will not require any form of security while based in the UK, many operate on the international arena and a large percentage do require some form of security service while abroad - especially if their business activity takes them into areas of greater risk than the UK. Once you have developed a business relationship with a client in the UK, he will almost certainly use you when he travels abroad. However, it is virtually unknown for a company or client to employ someone without a referral or recommendation. It just doesn't happen so don't try to market for that exclusive contract taking a client into Uzbekistan. Start at the bottom and work up, developing your reputation and credentials as you go.

TIP 1

The British and International Who's Who details almost every executive and celebrity worldwide. The British Woman's Who's Who, details all the major recognized and leading females in the UK. Most listings give their contact details, as well as their home address.

TIP 2

Subscribe to the top business magazines and journals: Business Life, Business Brief, Executive Women, Management Today etc, read through each issue carefully and contact those executives brokering major international deals and involved in major international conferences and negotiations. BP has just made the biggest investment in Russia by any company, ever. Can you imagine what contract tenders will be available in a few months' time?

TIP 3

Identify the top residential areas in the district where you live, obtain the Post Offices post code book and identify specific luxury houses. Send their occupants an introduction letter - properly addressed.

TIP 4

Read the daily broad sheet papers and note when a tragedy or crisis happens within the business community, e.g. last year's kidnapping and attempted extortion of a supermarket manager. Contact the head office concerned and offer your services.

TIP 5

Contact and introduce yourself to the minority action groups based in the UK e.g. Kurdish Peoples Party, Greenpeace etc. They may not need security but are constantly aware of the risk towards them and their members and one day might require your services. Also contact the top 500 charities, almost all of them have operations overseas and many use security. The Charity Directory lists over 5000 charities and humanity organizations with offices or representation in the UK.

TIP 6

Contact all the diamond and precious stone wholesalers and distributors - especially those that operate on the international arena. There are hundreds listed in the Thomson Business Guide CD. This guide also gives details of over 1 million businesses in the UK. This CD is available from Thomson's head office in Farnborough, Hants.

Again it is only your lack of imagination that will prevent you from developing your contact network. Think of every single possible way of introducing your company and the services you provide into the corporate arena.

Be highly suspicious of adverts asking for BGs. Nobody, ever, advertises for a BG. If you apply for an advert "BGs Wanted" you are normally being drawn into some sort of a scam, or someone is living in cloud coo coo land. There is enough of a network system to be able to easily and simply find the most professional and experienced BG without having to advertise in magazines or on web sites.

There are, however, some good international web sites were you can list you or your company for a relatively small annual fee. Sadly the ISE notice board has closed but it did occasionally reap those listed with lucrative contracts. It was a good way to meet and talk to other BGs and to network, which, as I have said time and time again, is what this industry is all about. If you are a security company, then for a small fee, you can list your details in The Varsity Directory of Security and Executive Protection (see page 95).

Warning - I have noticed that recently there have been adverts for so-called bodyguard agencies that offer to register bodyguards on their books for an administration fee. Fees can range from 20 GBP to over 100 GBP. There is NO NEED to pay an agency to register your details - no other employment agency in the UK charges personnel in this way, so nor should these security agencies. Agencies make their profit from a fee charged to companies when personnel are taken on from its database.

These are just a few tips and ideas for finding work, both within the corporate and celebrity sector. Most people, however, will refuse to do any of the above and still sit and wait for their 'phone to ring. Actually, it is good that most do sit and do nothing; it means that those who don't, who spend 10 hours a day 6 days a week fighting for business, will eventually succeed.

CASE HISTORY

While I was writing my first novel, an ex SAS friend of mine who now makes a very good living writing fiction novels called me and said, "Robin, if you write everyday, 6 days a week, 10 - 12 hours a day, you will eventually become successful".

Take that philosophy and you can't go wrong.

CHAPTER SEVEN

STARTING UP OVERSEAS

For most of you, this chapter is irrelevant but for the select few it will present you with possibly the very best opportunity you will ever have for getting work.

It is my philosophy that it is better to be one of a few than one of thousands. It is alleged there are over 10,000 BGs actively looking for work in the UK. In Moscow there are maybe three or four British BGs, so the prospect of me finding work will naturally be infinitely greater here in Moscow than in the UK. Added to this, being British and living within a close knit British expat community is the fastest and easiest way to network. We Brits stick together; we will almost always trust a fellow Brit over and above most Russians.

For the minority that really have no commitments in the UK, have some spare capital and really do want to work as a BG on the international arena, moving abroad and setting up business is an exciting, demanding, immensely challenging yet potentially highly profitable method of developing a selective, long term and loyal customer base. Plus it is possibly the best experience you might ever have.

Setting up abroad is not as hard as it sounds but there are conditions and logistical obstacles to overcome, and a lot of planning and thought. But in my opinion worth every penny and every problem.

SETTING UP OVERSEAS

Firstly it is important to choose a country that is at greater risk than the UK, otherwise there is no point in moving. To get an up-to-date country security risk rating look at www.airsecurity.com. South America, most of the ex Former Soviet States, most of middle Africa are classed at a risk factor of 4 or above.

The second condition is that there should be a good, prestigious and fairly large expat community in the country you are considering, not just UK residents but western Europeans in general. Turkmenistan, for instance, only has a few expats, but Uzbekistan, nearby, has far more and is marginally more open to foreign trade and relations. Trade Partners UK, at Victoria, London, has details of businesses registered abroad, or you can contact the British Embassy directly. Most major businesses register with the commercial department of the embassy of the country in which they are based.

So you have decided that you will set up a security consultancy service abroad. You have identified a country with a fairly large expat community with quite a lot of foreign trade. It is a country that is developing rapidly but still relatively poor and with a high crime rate. The Police are corrupt, the infrastructure is not that developed, yet there is vision for change and more and more foreign corporations - oil, banking, communications, transport, and mining - are expressing more and more interest in investing there.

Firstly, book a cheap flight and a cheap hotel and go for a week. Don't spend the week sightseeing - you should have time for that later when you move - but spend every waking minute meeting, networking and discussing possibilities for business with every foreigner you see. Go to the commercial department of the Embassy and find out about business clubs and meetings. They will give you a list of companies currently active, as well as details of those not yet established but planning to set up operations in the near future. Find out what investments are being made and in what sector and by whom. Go to every expat bar and nightclub.

Most countries will not allow you to work legally so in most cases you will have to set yourself up as a consultant only, a go-between. Do not violate the conditions of your visa - otherwise you could be deported. Most business visas will allow you to negotiate and discuss possible business co-operation. Make sure you have researched the conditions of your visa well and abide by those conditions - as much as you can!!!

You will also have to find a local provider of security services with whom you can feel comfortable working. A few letters and e-mails before you leave will set up connections and introductions.

Now you have to find somewhere to live. The best way is to contact the Embassy. Normally they can advise as to the best letting agents. However, most letting agents that deal with foreigners charge extremely high rates, as most foreigners have their accommodation paid for by their company. Unless, while you were in the country doing your research, you made contact with someone able to help, you will most likely have to go this route for the first few months until you eventually develop your own connections and find something a lot cheaper.

Apartments for foreigners in Moscow cost upwards of 1500 USD per month, apartments for Russians around 300 USD.

In almost every country there are web sites dedicated to matchmaking, friendship, love etc. For six or so months before you leave make as many contacts as possible via these web sites. Write to them and develop good strong friendships. They will help you find a suitable, cheap apartment even before you even arrive. Then all you need to do is pack and go, simple.

ONCE YOU ARRIVE.

TIP 1

Contact every western business listed with every western Embassy. Every Embassy has a commercial department dedicated to developing commercial ties between foreign and host country businesses, as well as between each other. Most Embassies will issue that list free of charge, or for a small fee. The American Embassy here in Moscow sells their list for around 50 USD, however that lists contains hundreds of companies and contacts and is worth every cent.

TIP 2

Join the British Chamber of Commerce attributed to that country. For instance the Russian - British Chamber of Commerce has membership from every major UK Corporation represented in Moscow. For the individual or small company it is quite expensive to join, but you will never otherwise have an opportunity to sip champagne on a balmy summer evening in gardens at the British Embassy with the chairman of an UK oil company, or take a boat trip sitting next to the director of one of the biggest accounting firms in the world. One of the major functions of the Chambers of Commerce is to put businesses together, and make introductions.

TIP 3

Join any British and European Business Club. The same applies as Tip 2.

TIP 4

Go to every single expat meeting. There are generally monthly business meetings in most Embassies, as well as other more social meetings in expat bars, clubs and hotels.

TIP 5

Hand your business card to each and every foreigner you come across - without exception. Don't force your business onto them, but just give them your card as a point of contact. I also give my card to any foreign tourists I come across and get talking to. A year or so ago I got chatting to an elderly American couple walking down a main street in Moscow, looking exactly like typical American tourists. He was a multi-millionaire, with manufacturing plants in four states in the US and homes in LA and Florida. Their ambition was to visit Moscow. They also came back the following year for another long weekend, and guess who they asked to show them around? A contact that you think might be useless just might not be!!

After a few short months you, and the services you provide, will be well known throughout the expat community. Any call for security consultancy will more than likely be immediately directed to you than to another non-British company. Believe me - it really does work.

If you lead an expat life, eat in expat restaurants and drink in expat bars, the cost of living will be the same as in the UK. Products for foreigners are generally imported and therefore cost as much, if not more than in the UK. However, if you want to immerse yourself within the local community in which you live, life can be cheap. If you rent an apartment, as the locals do, if you eat from the markets and kiosks or from the local supermarket, you can live very comfortably for immeasurably less than in the UK. This also means that, when starting up in business, you actually only need to earn a fraction of what you have to earn in the UK to have the same standard of living.

Having lived in Moscow for quite a while, I now have no desire to return to the UK to compete with every other BG for a relatively small percentage of business. There is simply no other Brit in Moscow with the experience I have and doing what I do. As we discussed in previous chapters, it is better to be acknowledged as a specialist than a generalist - and my speciality is providing a British managed high risk security and protection service for the corporate sector here in Moscow.

Why not do the same?

CHAPTER EIGHT

DIVERSIFYING

In an earlier chapter we discussed the advantages of being a specialist in one particular area of business rather than having a broad, but not a particularly detailed, knowledge of many areas. Let's look at other possible areas in which the recently qualified BG might like to specialize, and how these areas can be adapted and sold into the corporate world.

It could be, after a detailed market analysis and investigation, the main area of business in Russia, for instance, is not to provide a bodyguard service but investigations and surveillance. For the recently qualified BG, specializing will mean extensive and detailed further training, but if the market and money is there, the possibilities should be seriously considered.

SPECIALIZATION

Security Surveys and Evaluations
Providing companies and organizations with data and information gathered in the country or environment of origination. Providing on-site security surveys, breach of security analysis as well as making recommendations for improving security and safety.

Kidnap and Ransom
The huge increase in the kidnapping of expatriates as well as the high ransom demands, have made this specific area of business extremely profitable. Takes extensive training and experience but you get to work in some of the most volatile countries in the world.

Emergency Medicine
Providing international para-medicine and medical consultancy services for the corporate organization operating in high-risk environments. There are great and numerous opportunities for those from a Military Medical background, especially with the current situation in Iraq and Afghanistan.

Asset Protection
Many corporations and organizations need special security services in order to protect their key assets such as oil refineries, mining sites, harbours, power plants etc. Needs a strong and close working relationship with a good host security company, but contracts of this nature can be extremely profitable and long lasting.

International Charity and Aid Delivery
Many international aid agencies operate in high risk areas and in conflict zones. Many need specialized military style personal security services to keep their employees from harm and to ensure aid safely gets to its designated destination.

Corporate Security
Many international corporations need a high level of security at their HQ or production sites. Threats can come from a vast range of possible arenas - from the environmentalist wishing to damage property, to industrial espionage threatening financial instability.

Cash, Valuables and Document Protection
Important documents need to be delivered personally and safely around the world. Diamonds, gold, cash need to be transported safely to remote or hostile sites.

Training - Corporate
Many corporations prefer their own in-house security rather than employing a local outside contractor and require the skills of qualified and experienced training providers.

Training - Personal
Offering specialized safety and security training for CEO's and expatriates living overseas.

Training - Driving
Providing CEOs, higher management, chauffeurs and employees a concise offensive and defensive driver training service.

Surveillance and Investigations
Providing undercover surveillance of a corporation's own employees, if disloyalty is suspected, or a competitor's employees in order to gain a market edge.

Electronic Counter Measures
Espionage is a serious threat in today's competitive corporate world. ECM is needed in both offices and homes of many major corporations and organizations.

Asset Recovery
Investigating counterfeiting, fraud and lost assets.

Logistical Support
Providing the support services for a company setting up operation in a new territory.

There are many fields in which a security officer can specialize. If an area is of special interest then investigation in to the possibilities of further and specific training should be thoroughly researched. It may take a while to become a specialist, but the rewards are ultimately far greater than just being a "jack of all trades".

CHAPTER NINE

THE BODYGUARD'S CONTRACT OF EMPLOYMENT
THE CONTRACT

A contract of employment with either a security company or directly with a client himself must be clear, concise and to the point. A vaguely worded agreement is the same as no agreement at all. It should state clearly the job, working hours, payment, expenses, etc. There should always be room for movement, as circumstances and situations change, but a contract should be your working agreement with your contractor and should form the basis of the business relationship. An agreement should also give reasonable notice for the cancellation of the contract, and penalties and payments enforced, should reasonable notice not be given.

SAMPLE CONTRACT - amend and change according to your specific situation and task.

CONTRACT FOR PERSONAL PROTECTION

BETWEEN:

_____ hereinafter referred to as Bodyguard and

Company: _____

Represented by: _____

Address: _____

City: _____ Postcode: _____

Country: _____

1. Purpose of Agreement: Circumstances have led Client to believe that he, or other parties, are being targeted by criminal forces of some kind and he hereby agrees to contract with Bodyguard to provide personal protection services for himself and/or other parties for the length of time specified in this agreement.

2. Duration: This contract shall be for a period of

_____ to _____

Contract must be signed by both parties and will remain in force unless terminated under conditions listed in Paragraph 3.

3. Termination: This contract may be terminated under the following conditions:

(a) Agreement may be terminated by Client at any time, however, if less than _____ days notice is given a fee of _____ should be paid as compensation.

(b) Bodyguard is required to provide a _____ hour written termination notice.

4. Bodyguard fees (salary): Bodyguard is to be paid a salary of _____ per week; first week in advance.

IN ADDITION

a) The Bodyguard shall be paid living expenses as part of this contract.

b) The Client shall provide Bodyguard an extra weekly sum of _____ to pay incidental expenses that will be paid on Client's behalf; this shall include any and all travel expenses.

c) The Client agrees to pay Bodyguard, or his attorney, for other expenses incurred as a result of this contract as follows:

i) If during the course of his employment The Bodyguard is charged for any criminal/civil offence The Client will pay any expenses, including legal defence and any fines or judgments entered against Bodyguard. This is for charges incurred on behalf of The Client.

ii) If The Bodyguard is imprisoned (jailed) due to his employment with The Client, it is agreed that salary will continue to be paid at the same rate specified above.

5. Provision for Insurance: The Client agrees to provide the following insurance protection:

i) The Bodyguard will be provided with a term life insurance policy in the amount of One Million GBP / USD payable to The Bodyguard's beneficiary.

ii) plus major medical insurance for _____ coverage.

iii) this medical insurance to further provide disability provisions for a sum of _____

6. Duties Of Bodyguard: The Bodyguard agrees to make every effort and attempt to protect The Client or designated other parties from physical or bodily harm of any type. Client understands that The Bodyguard cannot guarantee the provisions of this paragraph and only promises to do every thing within his power.

7. Working Time Schedule: The Bodyguard's working hours shall be at The Client's convenience at anytime during each 24 hour period, although performance of duties will not exceed _____ hours at any one time without additional payment of _____ per hour worked.

8. The Client's Guarantee of Legality: It is agreed, without question, that The Bodyguard is unwilling to perform any duties that might be construed as being illegal, criminal or felonious. This applies to whatever locality in which duties may be performed.

9. Disclosure Guarantee: The Client, by signing this contract below, guarantees that all relevant information in regard to this contract for employment has been disclosed and any additional duties or responsibilities are not incumbent on The Bodyguard.

IN THE EVENT CLIENT FAILS TO HONOUR ANY OF THE ABOVE GUARANTEES IT WILL BE CAUSE FOR THE TERMINATION OF THIS AGREEMENT AND WAGES ARE DUE AND PAYABLE FOR THE TIME REMAINING ON CONTRACT.

10. Severability: If any portion, part or Paragraph of this contract should be judged illegal it is agreed by both parties that the rest will remain in force.

11. Legal Jurisdiction: The Client agrees that if The Bodyguard is forced to institute suit to enforce terms of this contract that the address provided on the first page of this contract will be considered the legal address, and the terms of this contract shall be applicable under the laws of the _____

12. Attorney's Fees: This contract includes all reasonable attorney fees and other costs in the event of litigation.

The above constitutes the entire agreement between The Client and The Bodyguard and no representations, guarantees or warranties have been made other than those specifically included herein.

Date: _____

Client's signature: _____

Bodyguard's signature: _____

Witness: _____

CHAPTER TEN

FREQUENTLY ASKED QUESTIONS
QUESTION

Is it good to be a member of any organization?

ANSWER

Certainly there are a few good organizations that are worth joining. I personally am a member of ASIS, IACSP and the IFPO. These are American organizations but with strong international links. Their newsletters are good and they are highly regarded within the security environment. ASIS has a chapter in the UK and most security managers of the big corporations are members of ASIS. They also run excellent specialized training programmes. The IFPO is mainly for serving US police and enforcement officers, and the IACSP publish an excellent quarterly magazine concentrating mainly on counter terrorism.

In the UK there is ASC, a good organization for security consultants, and the British Security Industry Association. The Professional Bodyguard Association and The International Bodyguard Association membership was restricted to those only who had attended their training courses. The WFB was sold to a subsidiary of Securitas in the year 2000 and has just re-started its individual membership programme open to anyone in the industry - regardless of training or experience. They produce a monthly newsletter, daily e-mail terrorist updates, cloth WFB badge for your training cap, certificate etc. Also they are probably one of the only organizations that contacts its members with details of contracts. Contact them at www.the-federation.com. There are a few other very small bodyguard associations and organizations but none that are particularly well known or recognized. In my opinion, the best organizations are those dedicated to the security industry in general and these are where most of the important and worthwhile contacts are made. Most security managers are members of the organizations listed, and these are the people you should be having contact with in order to find work.

QUESTION

Is it important to have a strong weapons training background?

ANSWER

No, absolutely not. Unless you are going into a Iraq or Afghanistan or into a war zone, it is extremely unlikely that you will ever be asked to carry a weapon. If you are contracted to work abroad you will closely co-operate with a host security team who will have all the necessary licences to carry firearms. As a foreigner, in most countries it is unlikely you will be granted authorization to carry a weapon anyway. There are a few exceptions but in general it will be illegal. Unless you have a strong military background, carrying a weapon will actually be more of a hindrance and, in some cases, down right dangerous. As I mentioned earlier, you should never say or do anything that you have no experience doing, and carrying a weapon without being totally proficient is stupid and reckless.

However, for your own interest and added skill, firearm training is a worthy addition to your portfolio of skills. In the UK it is virtually impossible to learn good basic firearm skills, but there are many other countries where firearm training is recognized and allowed, and a great deal of fun!!

QUESTION

How much do bodyguards earn?

ANSWER

How long is a piece of string? Friends of mine who are ex SAS wouldn't get out of bed for less than 500 GBP a day, more on international assignments. However, for the average BG on an average assignment in the UK, the average wage is around 200 - 250 GBP per day. For jobs abroad and depending upon the environment, from 350 GBP to 500 GBP per day. Long term permanent contracts, 50 - 80k GBP a year is the norm.

QUESTION

I have trained, I have skills but no actual hands on experience, and should I work for free or for a very low price just to get experience?

ANSWER

My first job I worked for a stupidly low wage patrolling a wet garden in Northern Ireland. I wanted the experience so I took the job. My bosses were please with my work and soon offered me another contract, with a marginally better pay packet.

Personally I almost always put new recruits into low paid jobs, just for experience. It is better to have a few low paid jobs in a portfolio than no jobs at all. However, it does not mean that you will forever work for a low wage.

Many bodyguards and BG companies cut their price down to the bare minimum just to get the job, and I think this is wrong. It is wrong to auction a contract to the lowest bidder. In my opinion, we deserve the money we get paid, and if you don't want to pay a good wage for a good job, then find someone less experienced, less well trained, less mature and hope to God he doesn't f**k up!!

QUESTION

Is it worth investing money advertising my company in magazines and journals?

ANSWER

I don't know of one contract that has been awarded to a company purely because of an advert in a magazine. There are places, such as the ISE website and Showcase Publications, where advertising your company is cheap and cost effective, but generally it is a waste of money putting adverts into magazines in order to just secure security contracts. Of course advertising in a specific magazine or journal for a specific service can be effective but general advertising for the BG business is not effective and is generally a waste of money. 95% of all business is by referral.

QUESTION

What security related magazines and periodicals do you suggest I read?

ANSWER

My favourites are INTERSEC, Counter Terrorism & Security International and Combat & Military. These three frequently cover the Close Protection industry. There are other good security related publications, such a Professional Security and Security Today, but they tend to concentrate more on the manned guard and equipment than close protection.

Jane's International produces an excellent series of publications including a weekly global terror alert. Expensive but worth every penny.

QUESTION

What is the best age to start a career in Close Protection, and what age can I work up to until I am considered "over the top?"

ANSWER

About a year ago I had an e-mail from a 20 year old. He asked at what age should he start training, and I said, NOW ! He was so excited, "Really?" he said, "you mean I can be a Bodyguard NOW?" "No", I said, "but you can start your training now. Go to a gym three times a week and get fit. Learn a good form of self defence, learn one, perhaps two languages, and call me in five year's time. Then you will be ready".

Any younger than 25 - 30 you will not have much credibility with employers and fellow team members. As for the upper age, well as long as you remain fit and healthy 45 - 50 seems to be the maximum.

QUESTION

How much should I reasonably expect to pay for a training course?

ANSWER

I have seen courses that range from 100 GBP to over 3000 GBP!! Most good weekend introduction courses can range from 150 to 300 GBP. Most good 6 - 10 day beginner's residential courses can range from 1000 to 2000 GBP which should include food and accommodation. Specialized courses can run from 100 GBP a day to thousands for a few weeks. Realistically most people pay an average of 1500 GBP to get their first basic training modules under their belt. I have known people to get work soon after their first course and make that investment back in a few short weeks. 1500 GBP really is not that much for what could potentially be a long, rewarding, exciting and possibly profitable career

QUESTION

Should I send my CV out to every single security company, or should I be selective?

ANSWER

Be selective. Many security companies do not provide BG services and it would be a complete waste of time and money sending your CV to them. Call them first. Ask if they have ever provided bodyguard services and if so could you send them your CV? By doing this you are again networking and again developing a database of possible contacts.

The same applies to corporations. Call the company first and ascertain who is responsible for security. Then call back and ask for him or her personally. If you made just 20 such calls a day, 5 days a week, in 3 months you will have a database of 1200 names and numbers.

QUESTION

Who are the main employers of Bodyguards?

ANSWER

Below are a number of UK and US companies that are known to employ a large amount of bodyguards. The 2004 Varsity Directory of Security and Executive Protection contains lists over 2000 names, addresses and contact details of companies in 110 countries worldwide as well as a detailed website directory. The price of the Directory is only 30GBP - a very cost effective way of obtaining valuable contacts worldwide. To purchase it contact Varsity Publications (see page 95).

CONTACT LIST
UK

AWE Stewarding and Security
Contact: A Chebib
9B Buckingham Rd, Brighton, BN1 3RA
Tel: + 44 1273 202704
Fax: + 44 1203 244425
E-mail: awe-uk@yahoo.com

Berkeley Security Bureau
MD: Mr M Bluestone
8-10 Grosvenor Gardens, London, SW1W 0DH
Tel: + 44 207 979 8833
Fax: + 44 207 979 8830
E-mail: bsbsecurity@compuserve.com

BCM Consulting
18 Weston Rd, Rochester, Kent, ME2 3EZ
Tel: + 44 1634 294 312
Fax: + 44 1632 295 799
E-mail: info@bcm-consulting.com
URL: www.bcm-consulting.com

Brigade Security
Contact: Danny Doyle
Suite 65, 2 Landsdowne Row, Berkeley Square, London, W1X 8HL

Bodyguard Protection
Proprietor: Mr M Faux
The Maltings, 98 Wilderspool, Warrington, WA4 6PS
Tel: + 44 1925 652 652
Fax: + 44 1925 652 525
E-mail: Mfaux@aol.com
URL: www.bodyguard-protection.com

Carnelian International Risks
PO Box 6933, Hatfield Peverelm, Chelmsford, CM3 2WF
Tel: +44 1245 380 698
Fax: +44 1245 382 894
Email: enquiries@carnelian-international.com

CAT VIP Escorts & Security
Contact: Chris Thomas
No 1 Candleston Newydd, Broadlands, Bridgend,
Mid Glamorgan, CF31 5DX
Tel/ Fax: + 44 1656 647037
E-mail: catvip@ukonline.co.uk
URL: www.catvip.com

C.A.W. Security
Contact: Bob Craft
9 Wimpole Street, London, W1M 8LB

Celebrity Protection Ltd
Director: Paul Dallanegra
Tel: + 44 191 259 1250
Fax: + 44 191 280 1749
E-mail: enquiries@celeb-protect.com

Chase Consultants
Contact: Mr P Consterdine
Unit 51, Chel Centre, 26 Roundway Rd, Leeds, LS7 1AB
Tel: + 44 113 242 9686
E-mail: chaseconsultants@compuserve.com

Control Risks Group
83 Victoria Street, London, SW1H 0HW

Drum Resources Ltd
39 Spring Street, London, W2 1JA
Tel: + 44 20 7706 2203
Fax: + 44 20 7706 2208

DSL Armorgroup
Eggington House, 25-28 Buckingham Gate, London, SW1
Tel: + 44 20 7808 5813
Fax: + 44 20 7828 2591

Events Management
Contact: Stephen Legg,
6 Quarry Park Close, Northampton, NN3 6QB
Tel: + 44 604 499 662
Fax: + 44 604 790 445

Exclusafe Security Consultants
Contact: Philip Moulton
14 Heywood Court, Manchester, M24 4RR
Tel + 44 161 654 8916
E-mail: Exclusafe@aol.com

Hart Risk Management
Contact: Mike Watson
60 Bromfelde Road, Stockwell, London SW4

ICP Group Ltd
Contact: Andy King
2 Old Brompton Rd, London, SW7 3DL

International Risk Control
Contact: Niall Burns,
2 Lansdowne Row, Berkeley Square, London, W1J 6HL
Tel: + 44 8700 702025
Fax: + 44 1202 496657
E-mail: enquiries@intriskuk.com

International Security Consultants
Proprietor: P Higgins
P.O. Box 96, Richmond, DL10 7YE
Tel: + 44 1748 826 592
E-mail: iseccon@supanet.com

Music and Arts Security
MD: Mr Jerry Judge
13 Grove Mews, Hammersmith, London, W6 7HS
Tel: + 44 208 563 9444
Fax: + 44 208 563 9555

Network International
26 Dover Street, London, W1X 4JU

Premier Entertainment Security
Director: Mr Garcia
154 White House, Albany St, London, NW1 3UU
Tel: + 44 207 387 9299
Fax: + 44 207 387 9299

Praetorian Special Projects Ltd
Director: Grant Osbourne
PO Box 229, Surrey, RH2 0YE
Tel: + 44 845 090 0145
E-mail: osbornepsp@cs.com

Protect 046 UK
Contact: Stephen Harris
PO Box 7, Amlwch, Gwynedd, LL68 9ZG
Tel: + 44 79 7172 4709
Fax: + 44 70 2116 6519

Brian Rix and Associates
Contact: Brian Rix
PO Box 100, Ashford, Kent, TN24 8AR
Tel: + 44 7010 700 800
Fax: + 44 7010 707 808

Rock Steady Security Ltd
Contact: Mark Hamilton,
93 Constitution St, Edinburgh, EH6 7AK
Tel: + 44 131 554 4400
Fax: + 44 131 554 3230

Saladin
7 Abingdon Road, Kensington High Street, London W8

Securicor - Special Events
Contact: Paul Bullen,
Gan House, 28 Dingwell Rd, Croyden, CR0 2NH
Tel: + 44 208 686 0123

Showsec International Ltd
Contact: Tony Ball,
Trinity House, Heather Park Drive, Wembley, HA10 1SU
Tel: + 44 208 903 3222
Fax: + 44 208 903 0322

Special Contingency Risks
85 Gracechurch Street, London, EC3V OHA

Squadron International
Contact: Richard Stanley
64 Knightsbridge, London, SW1X 7JF

Rubicon International Services
70 Upper Richmond Rd, Putney, London, SW15 2RP

Top Guard Sports and Leisure Security Services
169 High St, Loughton, IG10 4LF
Tel: + 44 208 502 5599
Fax: + 44 208 502 5512

Wynguard International
146 Clapham Manor Street, London, SW4 6BX

UNITED STATES OF AMERICA

American International Security Corporation
1 Boston Place, Suite 2650, Boston, MA 02108-4400
Tel: + 1 617 523 0523
Fax: + 1 617 367 4717
URL: www.aiscaol.com

American Protective Services Inc
Dwight Pederson,
7770 Pardee Lane, Oakland, CA 94621
Tel: + 1 510 568 0276

Barton Protective Services
CEO: Barton Rice
11 Piedmont Centre, Suite 410, Atlanta, GA 30305
Tel: + 1 404 266 1038
Fax: + 1 404 364 6373

Bureau of Diplomatic Security
U.S. Department of State, Washington, DC 20522
Tel: + 1 202 663 0533
Fax: + 1 202 663 0868
E-mail: osac@dsmail.state.gov

Centurion Protective Services Inc
Mr S White
122 North Elm Place, Broken Arrow, OK74012
Tel: + 1 918 251 2222
Fax: +1 918 251 0802
E-mail: cpss01@aol.com

Executive Outcome
CEO: Pasquale Di Pofi
P.O. Box 66204, Roseville, Michigan, MI 48066
Tel: + 1 810 725 3687
Fax: + 1 810 725 3123
E-mail: eo@i-is.com

Executive Protection Service
Albert C Zeller II,
819 Nassau Street, North Brunswick, NJ 08902
Tel: + 1 877 358 2611
E-mail: alzeller@executiveprotectionservice.net

Executive Security International (ESI)
Gun Barrel Sq, 2128 Railroad Ave, Rifle, Oolorado, CO 81650
Tel: + 1 970 625 9000
Fax: + 1 970 625 9044
E-mail: esi@esi-lifeforce.com

Global Threats Protective Services
Contact: Juan A. Garcia
219a Jamul Lane, Oceanside, CA 92054
Tel: + 1 760 430 8178
E-mail: garciajag@hotmail.com

Imperial Protective Service
15849 N. 71st Street, Suite #100, Scottsdale, Arizona, AZ 85254
Tel: + 1 602 390 0813
E-mail: marketing@executiveprotect.com

Kroll Associates
CEO: Jules Kroll
900 Third Ave, New York, NY 10022
Tel: + 1 212 833 3236
Fax: + 1 212 644 5794

New York Security Service
Stephen Marrone
734 Franklin Ave, Suite #693, Garden City, NY 1530
Tel: + 1 516 248 8557
Fax: + 1 516 248 8557
E-mail: bodygard@optonline.net

Mid West Protective Services
Tim Flora
1374 Clarkson Centre, Suite 338, St Louis, MO 63011
Tel: + 1 314 391 2188
Fax: + 1 314 227 3155
E-mail: mid-west@earthlink.net

Pinkerton Consulting
MD: Scott Jenkins
39825 Paseo Padre Park, Fremont, CA 94538
Tel: + 1 510 656 2626
Fax: + 1 510 656 6790

Protection & Investigation Services Corp
Mr. W. Masterson
PO Box 6182, Stuart, FL 34997
Tel: + 1 866 301 8111
Fax: + 1 772 223 8945
E-mail: batm007@aol.com

Security Professionals Inc
Mr Franklin Hirst, 5639
56th Terrace North, St. Petersburg, FL 33709
Tel: + 1 727 544 7380
Fax: + 1 727 545 8639
E-mail: Fhirst@tampabay.rr.com

The Slavin Group
Contact: Zachary Slavin
814 Washington Street, Baldwin, NY 11510
Tel: + 1 516 713 5800
E-mail: info@slavin.com

Wackenhut
Mr R Wackenhut,
4200 Wackenhut Dr, Palm Beach Gardens, Florida, FL 33410
Tel: + 1 561 622 5656
Fax: + 1 561 662 7439

Vance International
10467 White Granite Drive, Oakton, Virginia, VA 22124
Tel: + 1 703 385 6754
Fax: + 1 703 359 8456
E-mail: info@vancesecurity.com

HAPPY JOB HUNTING!!

Why not join the Worldwide Federation of Bodyguards?

Regardless of training or experience, the new WFB International Membership is open to ANYONE in the industry. The aim of membership is to unite and bring together bodyguards the world over, both veterans with many years experience, and the novice who has yet to fulfil his / her first contract. Unlike most other organisations, conditions of membership do **NOT** depend upon training with the WFB; membership is open to **ANYONE** in the business. Our philosophy is to unite, develop and educate through contact with others in the industry and around the world. From Nigeria to the Philippiness, from Russia to the UK and the US, WFB Members will form one vast network of like-minded professionals.

Membership costs just 35 GBP a year. To join or to receive full details contact: TheWFB@aol.com.
or telephone +44 7932 637738
or write: The WFB c/o Robin Barratt, Unit 56, 3 Courthill House, 60 Water Lane, Wilmslow, SK9 4AJ, Great Britain.

WORLD-WIDE FEDERATION OF BODYGUARDS

Varsity International Directory of Investigators

Editor: Stuart Bridges

About Varsity
Varsity Publications has been producing its specialist Directories for over 20 years and is now firmly established as the most useful and reliable source of information of this type.

About The Directory
The Varsity International Directory of Investigators is published every two years and the latest edition contains **300 pages** packed with vital information on over **2000 Investigators** in **150** Countries worlwide.

This year the Directory is bigger and better than ever before, with **more** companies, **more** Display Advertisers, **more** Countries listed and more information. There are maps showing all the Countries covered, **plu**s an information panel for each one giving vital details such as local currency and time-differences etc.

The **Varsity Directory** also enjoys the support and involvement of almost all National and International Professional Associations worldwide, such as the World Association of Detectives, the World Association of Professional Investigators, the World Investigators Network, the Association of British Investigators and the Institute of Professional Investigators.

About The Editor
The Varsity Directory is Edited by Stuart Bridges, BA, Member of the Association of British Investigators, who ran his own successful Investigation business in the UK for over 20 years before concentrating entirely on publishing specialist books for Investigators, Security Companies and the Legal Profession.

How to Order
This Directory costs just **£35.00** sterling (approx **US$60** - including Air Mail postage & packing anywhere in the world).

We accept payment by **VISA**, **Mastercard** or **American Express**. Please send us details of your credit card number and expiry date, **OR** please enclose your cheque for **£35.00** sterling made payable to **Varsity Publications**.

Please mail to:
Varsity Publications, PO Box 222, Chipping Norton, Oxford OX7 5WY, UK
or Fax: **++ 44 (0)870 - 350 1241** or e-mail to: **varsityox@aol.com**

Please give your name and full mailing address, together with your complete contact details if you would like to be included in the next edition of the Directory.

International Directory of Security & Executive Protection

Out Now!

The latest edition of the **INTERNATIONAL DIRECTORY OF SECURITY & EXECUTIVE PROTECTION** lists over **2000** contacts in **110** countries worldwide, as well as almost 1000 web site addresses and details of literally hundreds of terrorist groups - giving you instant access to the global executive protection and security arena.

"More contacts in this industry than I have ever found anywhere else", Pat Rogers — PR Protection, Maidenhead.

The only Directory of its kind in the world and unparalleled in its range of information, it details executive protection and security companies, consultants, armoured vehicles and and body armour providers, celebrity protection providers, limousine and private aircraft hire, training providers, security associations and more.....

Compiled by R. Barratt and published by Varsity Publications, Oxford, UK.

How to Order
This Directory costs just **£30.00** sterling (approx **US$55** - including Air Mail postage & packing anywhere in the world).

We accept payment by **VISA, Mastercard** or **American Express**. Please send details of your credit card number and expiry date, **OR** please enclose your cheque for **£30.00** sterling made payable to **Varsity Publications**.

Please mail to:
Varsity Publications, PO Box 222, Chipping Norton, Oxford OX7 5WY, UK
or Fax: **++ 44 (0)870 - 350 1241** or e-mail to: **varsityox@aol.com**

Please give your name and full mailing address, together with your complete contact details if you would like to be included in the next edition of the Directory

Varsity Directory of Investigators and Process Servers

Published annually since 1984, this is **the** definitive guide to the services offered by professional investigators, process servers, bailiffs, security consultants, etc. throughout the U.K. and Ireland.

Over 1,200 entries are classified geographically and list names, addresses, telephone, fax, DX and e-mail numbers, together with the type of services offered and to which professional bodies the organisation or individual belongs. 100% of the entries have been verified and updated as necessary.

In addition to the geograhical listings, a Postcode Index makes it even easier to find the right company for your needs.

Within the directory's pages will be found numerous additional services of immense value to the legal profession, courts and other professionals.

ISBN 0 7219 1575 2   **A5 paperback**
£32.00, post free in the UK (£35 overseas)

Selected entries from this directory are available free on the internet at www.varsityinvestigators.co.uk

Send Cheques or Credit Card details to:

**Shaw & Sons Limited, Shaway House, 21 Bourne Park,
Bourne Road, Crayford, Kent DA1 4BZ
Tel. 01322 621111
Fax. 01322 550553
E-mail: sales@shaws.co.uk**